HOW TO
BIRDWATCH

HOW TO
BIRDWATCH

STEPHEN MOSS

NEW HOLLAND

This edition first published in 2006 by New Holland Publishers (UK) Ltd
London • Cape Town • Sydney • Auckland
www.newhollandpublishers.com

Garfield House, 86–88 Edgware Road, London W2 2EA
80 McKenzie Street, Cape Town 8001, South Africa
14 Aquatic Drive, Frenchs Forest, NSW 2086, Australia
218 Lake Road, Northcote, Auckland, New Zealand

10 9 8 7 6 5 4 3 2 1

ISBN 1 84537 457 6

Publishing Manager: Jo Hemmings
Project Editor: Camilla MacWhannell
Cover Design: Gülen Shevki-Taylor
Design: Wildlife Art Ltd / John Hughes
Production: Joan Woodroffe

Reproduction by Modern Age Repro Co., Hong Kong
Printed and bound in Malaysia by Times Offset (M) Sdn Bhd

Photographs appearing on pages 6-7 are as follows:
Page 6: Male Dartford Warbler (top left); Gannets (centre left); Titchwell RSPB
Reserve, Norfolk (bottom). Page 7: Marsh Harrier (top right); Male Capercaillie
(centre right).

Photographic Acknowledgements

All the photographs in this book were taken by David Tipling except for the
following:
RSPB: Chris Gomersall (p10); Malcolm Hunt (p52); Andy Hay (p86, p88, p92);
Steve Austin (p87 & back cover).
David Cottridge: p107 (top)

Artwork Acknowledgements

All the artworks in this book are by David Daly except for the following by
Stephen Message:
p45, p47 (top and centre), p48, p64, p67, p75 (bottom), P80, p81, p82, p93,
p100, p101.

THE WILDLIFE TRUSTS

The Wildlife Trusts partnership is the UK's leading voluntary organisation working, since 1912, in all areas of nature conservation. We are fortunate to have the support of more than 366,000 members, including some famous household names.

The Wildlife Trusts protect wildlife for the future by managing in excess of 2,300 nature reserves, ranging from woodlands and peat bogs, to heath lands, coastal habitats and wild flower meadows. We campaign tirelessly on behalf of wildlife, including of course the multitude of bird species.

We run thousands of events, including dawn chorus walks and birdwatching activities, and projects for adults and children across the UK. Leicestershire and Rutland Wildlife Trust, with the RSPB, organises the British Birdwatching Fair at Rutland Water – now also home to Osprey. The Wildlife Trusts work to influence industry and government and also advise landowners.

As numbers of formerly common species plummet, we are urging people from all walks of life to take action, whether supporting conservation organisations in their work for birds, or taking a few small steps in their own lives.

Whilst many birders choose to explore every corner of the British Isles, and beyond, for many novices the local park or back garden can provide a good starting point and be just as enjoyable.

And it is for these beginners to birdwatching that *How to Birdwatch* is such an excellent introduction. Stephen Moss conveys the enjoyment experienced whether simply birding in the garden and your local patch, or venturing farther afield on an organised excursion. The book is also a valuable resource for conservation and how you can help today's bird life, whether by taking part in a BTO census or one of the many Wildlife Trust projects.

A recent survey conducted by The Wildlife Trusts, in association with the Daily Telegraph and BBC's Tomorrow's World, asked people to tick off the wildlife they had seen in their garden over the previous year. The list included the Robin, Blackbird, Wren and House Sparrow. More than 66,000 people responded, confirming what experts had warned, for example that the House Sparrow had declined dramatically. Results also told us just how much people love watching wildlife, especially birds.

The Wildlife Trusts is a registered charity (number 207238). For membership, and other details, please phone The Wildlife Trusts on 0870 0367711, or log on to www.wildlifetrusts.org

CONTENTS

INTRODUCTION

When I began watching birds, as a child in the early 1970s, I had to rely on just a handful of bird books. The one that started me off was *The Observer's Book of Birds*, which, even then, was more than thirty years old, and showing its age. I then graduated to the famous *Peterson, Mountfort and Hollom* field guide, the Bible for my generation of birders.

I also had the excellent *Reader's Digest Book of British Birds*, a lavish, coffee-table work with wonderfully vivid illustrations by the New Zealand bird artist Ray Harris Ching. And I was an avid reader of John Gooders' *Where to Watch Birds*. This well-thumbed little book described 500 or so of the best places to watch birds in Britain, from Scilly to Shetland, and West Wales to East Anglia. It held out all sorts of tantalising possibilities, although as I soon discovered, the reality of a day out at one of the prime sites did not always live up to the description in the book!

The one book I did not have was a book on *how* to watch birds. Even if I had, I'm not sure that I would have paid it much attention. Like most new birders, I was impatient to see more and more new species, and would rather look through page after page of my field guide than actually learn new techniques which might have made me a better birder.

So I mostly fended for myself, and as a result made an awful lot of mistakes. In some ways that was a good thing: like learning anything from languages to cookery, a long apprenticeship does pay dividends in the end, even if it seems frustrating at the time. Now, thirty years after I started to watch birds, I sit down to write this book. I have tried to cast my mind back to that eager eleven-year-old, and remember what he would have wanted from such a work.

Redwing

I also have in mind the many other new birders I have met over the years, aged from eight to eighty, all of whom had one thing in common: they were eager to learn everything they could about this fascinating subject.

Some, though keen at first, have fallen by the wayside, and in doing so have passed up a golden opportunity to embark on what one birder has called 'a lifetime's consuming passion'. Others may still be hanging on in there: confused by ducks in eclipse plumage, gulls in flight, or the myriad 'little brown jobs' that plague the new birder. Don't despair! Although this book will not solve all your problems, it will guide you through some of the pitfalls of your new-found hobby, and, with luck, enable you to gain confidence, and progress a little more quickly than you might otherwise have done.

Male Blackcap

How to Birdwatch will guide you through the 'fieldcraft' of watching birds, enabling you to find, observe and learn about birds for yourself. It will open your eyes to the passion, the thrills, the disasters, the humour – and, above all, the sheer enjoyment – of birding.

Throughout, I have used anecdotes from my own and other people's experiences to illustrate various points. Where possible, I have tried to give specific examples when talking about a particular problem. And to help you, I have condensed some key points into 'top tips' – if you can't be bothered to read the whole book, at least look at these!

Finally, I wish you luck. It is no exaggeration to say that for me, birding has guided the course of my life, and given it some of its structure and meaning. Sure, there are all sorts of other important things – family, friends, music, art, sport, television, books, and so on. Birding belongs in the same category as all these: something that ultimately makes life worth living. So go on – have a go! You won't regret it.

1 GETTING STARTED

Birdwatchers are not, by inclination, a philosophical bunch, and if you ask them why they watch birds, they are likely to give you an answer equivalent to the mountain climber's 'because it's there'. Perhaps the most obvious reason is that birds are by far the most visible and accessible of all living creatures: easier to see than mammals, less seasonal than butterflies and moths, less confusing than wild flowers. They come in a variety of shapes and sizes, and can be seen more or less anywhere, from the centre of a city to a remote offshore island, and virtually everywhere in between. Birdwatching gets you out in the open air – I've certainly been to many places I wouldn't ever have visited if I hadn't been looking for birds. And there's the element of challenge: birds can be hard to see, and even more difficult to identify.

WHY WATCH BIRDS?

But there's a lot more to birding than that. There's the social side of the hobby: many people have made lifelong friends, and in my case a lifelong partner, through their shared passion for birds. On the other hand, it can be a way to escape from the hurly-burly of the world: there's nothing more relaxing than simply wandering around on your own, enjoying the sights and sounds of birds, and dreaming of stumbling across something rare or unexpected.

On a deeper level, as you watch birds you begin to get a privileged insight into their daily lives, and as your knowledge builds you start to see the world differently. From an altruistic point of view, by watching birds we (hopefully) help to conserve them for future generations.

But although all these are perfectly valid reasons for watching birds, there is still something missing. I can only describe it as a spiritual, almost religious dimension, which marks off the true birder from the person who has only a passing interest. A word of warning here: birding is like a drug, and once you're hooked, there's no going back. In *Fever Pitch*, Nick Hornby's wonderful book on what it means to be a football fan, he wonders what life would be like if his dad had taken him to a museum or the zoo instead of to watch Arsenal when he was an impressionable youngster. He finds the whole prospect of life without football too horrific even to contemplate.

Birding gets you out in the fresh air – and leads to lifelong friendships too!

Birding is like that: ask any birder what their life would have been like if they hadn't started watching birds and they find it impossible to imagine. Birding is all-encompassing in its scope, and can be enjoyed in so many different ways. Perhaps the best description of the motivation for birding was written by James Fisher, back in 1940:

'The observation of birds may be a superstition, a tradition, an art, a science, a pleasure, a hobby, or a bore; this depends entirely on the nature of the observer'.

He was right – and if you want to add any other word to his list, such as sport, delight or obsession, you are most welcome. Ultimately, birding is whatever you want it to be!

FIRST STEPS

What do you need to watch birds? Well according to many early writers on the subject: a good pair of eyes and ears, a keen sense of curiosity, and perhaps a notebook to write things down, were the only tools required.

Most, if not all, modern birders couldn't imagine going birding without one other essential piece of equipment: a pair of binoculars. And they're right. Looking through a good pair of 'bins' is like putting your eyes through a spring-clean: you can see details you've never seen before, opening up a whole new world of appreciation.

If you don't believe me, try walking round your local park without binoculars, and write down what you see.

Then take the same walk with a pair of binoculars. The difference in quality of experience simply by looking through an optical aid, is quite extraordinary.

A good pair of binoculars lets you into the birds' own world – giving close-up views of this pair of Green Woodpeckers.

For at its heart, birding is primarily about aesthetics. You can't really begin to appreciate a bird until you see it close up; until you enter its world and discover for yourself how it looks and behaves. So yes, without question, binoculars are a vital tool of the trade.

What else do you need? Well, to be honest, you could stop there. By the standards of most hobbies, such as photography or cycling, birding is pretty cheap. Indeed, your initial investment can be as little as £100, which will get you a battered but decent pair of second-hand binoculars, a notebook, and a basic field guide.

Later on, you can spend a fortune if you wish, but it won't necessarily improve the quality of your experience. I am quite convinced that most birders who rarely venture away from their local patch can enjoy more satisfying experiences than many 'world listers' – the tiny band of very rich, mostly American people who travel the globe in order to tick off every one of its

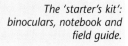

The 'starter's kit': binoculars, notebook and field guide.

ten thousand or so species. Fortunately for those of us not blessed with unlimited financial resources, they don't always appear to enjoy it very much!

So for now, equipped with eyes, ears, notebook, field guide and binoculars, you can have just as much fun, interest and enjoyment as any well-travelled birder, providing you have the right attitude – one of appreciative curiosity!

CHOOSING AND USING BINOCULARS

Watching birds without binoculars is like eating a three-course meal without cutlery: it can be done, but you wouldn't recommend it. Owning a pair of binoculars opens up a whole new world, allowing you to begin to really appreciate the beauty and fascination of birds for the very first time.

Binoculars come in all shapes and sizes: including traditional 'porro-prism' (centre) and the newer 'roof-prism' designs (left and right). Roof prisms tend to be more expensive.

If you're a beginner, binoculars are likely to be the first major financial outlay of your new hobby, costing anything from under £100 to almost £1,000. At that price, mistakes can be expensive. Fortunately there are a whole range of excellent binoculars on the market, with a pair to suit every pocket. However, it is worth saying that the more you pay the more likely you are to get a model with higher quality optics, and a better build, which will last you longer. But as with all consumer products, there are always exceptions to this rule.

So where should you go to buy them? First of all, avoid newspaper offers, high street shops and market stalls. Most of the bins on offer are about as much use as something out of a Christmas cracker, and a lot more expensive. Instead, go to one

top tip

GET SOME BINOCULARS

Beg, buy or borrow the very best pair of binoculars you can. Until you've looked at birds through a decent pair of bins you just don't know what you're missing. Good optics open up a whole new world of colour, plumage detail and behaviour.

13

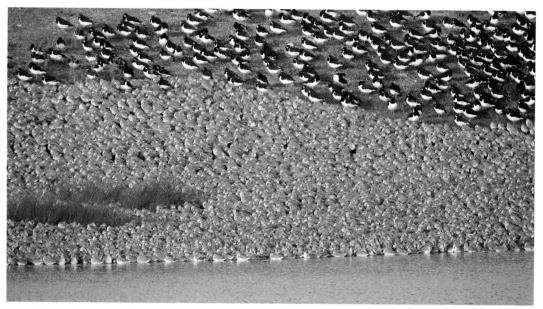

Without binoculars a flock of waders just looks like a mass of birds, though the Oystercatchers (top) can still be identified.

top tip

PICK UP A BARGAIN

If you have a limited budget, check out second-hand models from a specialist retailer. Some birders change their bins every time a new model appears, so you can sometimes pick up a bargain.

of the specialist optical traders who advertise in the pages of monthly birding magazines, and don't be afraid to ask advice. A good retailer will always sell the right pair for you, not the one he's trying to get rid of!

Remember, with binoculars, size really doesn't matter. Beginners often make the mistake of choosing the heaviest pair with the highest magnification. But high magnification alone does not guarantee quality of image, and the higher the power, the harder it is to keep a steady hold. Far better to have a clear, bright, small image than a fuzzy, dull, big one.

People talking about binoculars often refer to what sounds like a multiplication sum, such as 8 x 30, or 10 x 50. The first figure is the magnification, or power, and the second is the diameter in millimetres of the objective lens (the big one at the front). By and large, the lower the magnification the better the light-gathering power, and the wider the field of view, making it easier to locate small, fast-moving birds in dense foliage. However, models do vary considerably, so make sure you give them a thorough 'test-drive' before buying.

For birding, your best bet is probably 8x, though if you often go out at dawn and dusk you may prefer a 7x model, while if you spend most of your time on marshes or reservoirs, where the birds are distant, 10x is more suitable. If you use a telescope as well, you can get away with a lower magnification.

Once you've decided what you can afford, then try out several pairs in that price-range. Concentrate on how they feel for you: especially the weight, and how easy you find them to hold and focus. Different binocular designs suit different people, so don't just go by what a friend or the salesperson says. Most important of all, compare them by looking through the lenses. Is the image sharp and clear, right to the edge? Are the colours true to life? Can you see any strange lines or strobe effects?

Another important factor is depth of field. Some models have a very small depth of field, but the advantage that it only takes maybe half a turn of the focusing wheel to change from close to distant focus. Others have a much greater depth of field, but it may take two or more turns to go from close-up to far away. Personally I prefer those with a greater depth of field, but everyone has their own preferences.

Finally, check the close-focusing, especially if you enjoy watching dragonflies and butterflies as well as birds. Some models focus down to just two or three metres, while others perform far less well – which can be frustrating when the bird of your dreams pops up right in front of you!

Once you've chosen your binoculars, then look after them. Clean the lenses regularly: first with a soft photographer's brush to remove grit and dust, then with a lens tissue. Some people avoid lens-cleaning fluid, but I find it's the only way to shift the dirt and grease that inevitably accumulates. Some of the more expensive models are completely sealed, so that they can even be washed under a tap – but make sure you check this out first!

Out in the field, practise quick focusing, and the technique of finding a bird through the lens as quickly as possible. Adjust the eyepieces to fit your particular sight, and learn to hold the binoculars with the minimum of shake. Soon you'll find they have become an extension of your own eyesight, and the pleasures of birding can really begin.

Binoculars help you tell similar species apart: revealing the orange legs of the Ringed Plover (above), and the distinctive yellow eye ring of the Little Ringed Plover (left).

MAKING NOTES

Next to your binoculars, a notebook is probably your most essential piece of equipment. If you want to make progress in your ability to identify birds it's absolutely vital to learn how to make field notes. Indeed, being able to make detailed, accurate notes is one of the fundamental skills of birding.

Field notes can do much more than simply help you identify an unfamiliar species. They may enable you to work out a bird's age and sex, and understand any unusual or distinctive behaviour. They serve not just as an immediate account of the bird, but as a permanent record of your experiences in the field.

Which kind of notebook you use is a matter of personal choice: some people prefer a loose-leaf version, others a standard one. Just make sure it can fit in your pocket and is tough enough to stand up to life in the field; perhaps with a water-resistant cover for those days when the weather turns bad!

Making field notes and sketches takes time and practice, but will help you improve your identification skills and understanding of bird behaviour.

As an alternative to pen and paper, you can use a miniature tape-recorder, as I do. This has advantages and disadvantages. The upside is that you don't have a problem deciphering unreadable handwriting, and, in winter, your fingers don't get frozen. Also, you can speak faster than you can write, enabling you to get the important details down quickly, while still looking at the bird.

The downside is that the battery may go flat just as you're watching the bird of a lifetime. Or you may press 'play' instead of 'record', or accidentally erase a whole description by recording over it. Finally, you do have to spend time transcribing the material when you get home.

Even if you can't draw, a quick outline of the bird noting shape, markings and bill length, will be invaluable for a later identification.

Whichever method you decide to use, however, the procedure for taking notes stays the same. The golden rule is to make sure you get down the essential points straightaway. Don't waste time taking down details of the bird's habitat, weather conditions, or the date and time of the sighting – all these can wait until after the bird has flown off.

Instead, concentrate on the essentials: starting with size and shape (comparing the bird with similar, familiar species), then its overall appearance, or 'jizz'. As soon as you can, note down the plumage details.

There are exceptions to this rule, however. If you think the bird is about to fly away, or it is only giving brief or partial views, then pay attention to the key ID (identification) points. Don't spend time writing a feather-by-feather description of the wing if you know that for this particular group of species, head-pattern or leg-colour are more important features. So if you're looking at an unusual gull, concentrate on its bill, legs, and back colour; all key factors in gull identification. For a wader, length and shape of its bill are important.

It's also worth learning the basics of 'bird topography' – the external features and feather-patterns of a bird (*see* p37). This will enable you to describe what you see in precise, accurate terms, rather than using vague, all-embracing words like 'wing' or 'underparts'. For some species, a cast-iron identity can only be established if the description includes specific terms like 'primaries' or 'lores'.

For many species, especially groups of similar-looking birds like warblers, calls and song are important clues to identification. Writing an accurate description of these can be difficult, as there are no exact human equivalents to bird vocalisations. Try to capture the rhythm, tone and melody of the sounds you hear – perhaps using diagrams rather than words.

The bird's habits are often another important clue to its identity. Try to describe what it is doing, perhaps in comparison with other species nearby. Don't be afraid to use simile or metaphor: once you've seen a Sanderling running along the tideline 'like a clockwork toy' you realise why it is such a perfect description.

In flight Stonechats can be confused with Whinchats. Look for the white patch on the wing and note the lack of white on the tail edges.

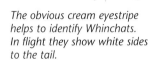

The obvious cream eyestripe helps to identify Whinchats. In flight they show white sides to the tail.

One birder I know learned to distinguish Sand Martin from House Martin by looking for the band on its chest. She remembered the distinguishing mark by using the fact that 'band' rhymes with 'sand'. Everyone has their own method of remembering a particular species: so use whatever works for you!

Sand Martins are the smallest of all the Hirundines; their flight is rather weak compared to other members of the Swallow family.

If you can, do a quick sketch of the bird. However bad your drawing skills (and mine are truly awful!), it will at least help you to pinpoint the key field marks, using arrows.

Finally, take a note of the date and time, habitat, direction and quality of light, and the weather conditions. If appropriate, add details of other observers present. If you're submitting the record to the local bird recorder, or the national Rarities Committee, they will expect you to include these background details.

The deeply-forked tail of the Swallow is a good aid to identifiction.

One word of warning: when taking field notes it's always tempting to write down something you think you saw, or expected to see. Don't. If you didn't see the bird's leg colour, say so. And whatever you do, don't try to 'fill in the gaps' by referring to field guides. Many a good description has been rejected by a records committee because it was a little too detailed.

The all-white underparts and short forked tail of the House Martin distinguish it from its close relatives.

Finally, keep your field notebooks safe. You'll be surprised how enjoyable it is to pick them up a few years later, and re-read your accounts of memorable days in the field.

FIELD GUIDES

Apart from binoculars and a field notebook, a field guide is probably your most essential piece of equipment. Yet despite this, using a field guide presents a whole range of potential pitfalls, and may even slow down your progress as a birder.

Your first problem is choosing which guide is the right one for you. Some only cover the birds of the British Isles, others the whole of the Western Palearctic, from Iceland to Iraq, and

If you are planning a birding trip abroad, getting the right field guide is essential.

Norway to Morocco. Some have the text and illustration on facing pages, for easy access; others have plates showing many similar species, with the description elsewhere. Some are pocket-sized, with rows of tiny, thumbnail portraits of birds you need a magnifying glass to see; others are so heavy you could use them as a doorstop.

Even when you've chosen the guide, and taken it into the field, your troubles aren't over. Field guides either show you all the birds in one position (the Peterson method, named after the pioneering American bird artist Roger Tory Peterson), or each species in a different pose from another (favoured by, for example, Lars Jonsson). Both have their drawbacks. The first allows close comparison between similar species, but can be poorly-suited to viewing birds in actual field situations. The second is more lifelike, but makes a thorough comparison between two similar species more difficult.

But without doubt, the biggest drawback of field guides is the 'it must be a...' syndrome. Just as every UFO sighting will

top tip

FIND A FRIEND

Birdwatching can be pretty frustrating at times – especially when you just can't identify the birds you see. So why not find a friend who's just started birding too, to share your growing interest. Better still; join up with a more experienced birder, who can act as your 'mentor'.

At first sight this bird may appear confusing, as its plumage may not be featured in your field guide. In fact it is a juvenile Starling beginning to acquire adult plumage.

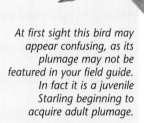

Compared to adult Puffins, juveniles have a grey wash to the cheeks and more subdued bill colour.

The white breast band on male Ring Ouzels, seen clearly when in full breeding plumage (far right) and less so in first winter (bottom), make this species unmistakable. Females (top) have a much less obvious band but have heavily-scaled underparts.

produce a string of copycat reports, so having a picture of a bird in front of your eyes can cause you to hallucinate. Every birder has said those fatal words: 'it looked just like the picture in the book, so it must be a…' Sometimes it's not. Field guides are not Holy Writ, and birds can look very different from normal, depending on factors such as the light and the weather conditions. So be warned!

Indeed, some experienced observers consider that field guides actually retard a birder's progress in identifying birds. They maintain, with some justification, that only by closely looking at every bird you see can you really learn how to identify birds for yourself. Remember that noting the differences between members of the same species can be just as important as understanding the similarities between birds of different species.

But there can be no doubt that field guides have made tremendous progress in the last thirty years or so, since I tried to

identify waders using Thorburn's antiquated illustrations in *The Observer's Book of Birds*. We are now getting pretty close to the ultimate field guide, which would show every possible plumage of every different species; show birds in every possible position, especially flying away from the observer; and would give you instant access to text and illustration, so the bird didn't disappear while you're looking it up.

There's only one problem: the ideal field guide would be the size of a small encyclopaedia, and give you a hernia if you tried to carry it. Perhaps in a few years time, technology will have caught up, and we'll all be using small hand-held computers to identify the birds we see. Until then, you'll just have to rely on existing field guides, and our own ability to sort out the wheat(ear) from the (chiff)chaff! Just make sure you look closely at the real bird before you look it up in the book!

When in doubt, a field guide can provide much needed help with identification, but don't be too reliant on it.

CLOTHING

In autumn, as the temperature begins to drop, and the days grow shorter, a birder's mind turns towards the vexed subject of what to wear in the field. It's not so much a fashion decision, as a practical one: which clothes will keep the cold, wind and rain out, while enabling you to be mobile without overheating?

The problem is that birding is neither an entirely sedentary pastime, like fishing, nor mainly active, like mountain-climbing; but one punctuated by stops and starts. Birders spend much of the time walking, during which the body overheats. But once they stop and stay put for a while, for example in a hide, the body rapidly begins to chill. This soon leads to discomfort, and in extreme cases, can spoil a good day out.

So what can be done about the problem? One answer is to cast off the traditional birder's garb of cotton T-shirts, woolly jumpers and heavy waxed jackets, and take a tip from the climbing fraternity. Go to any reputable outdoor activity shop, and you'll be confronted with a bewildering array of clothes, many of them in unsuitably bright colours. But don't be put off by first impressions – most items come in more muted colours, better suited to birding.

The key to the new approach to staying warm and dry is recent advances in man-made fabrics. These work by being 'breathable', allowing any interior moisture to be wicked away, so avoiding chills. The usual approach is to wear a thin thermal layer next to the skin, covered with one or more fleeces – the man-made equivalent of a woolly jumper.

Fleeces trap warm air while also removing moisture, and come in a variety of weights, each suited to different conditions.

Winter is a great time to watch woodland birds, especially during hard weather – but make sure you wrap up warm!

It is difficult to know exactly what to wear for the average day's birding in the UK. The best thing to do is wear thin layers that can be easily removed: a fleece for warmth, a raincoat for protection and a hat for all seasons.

However, they are not always windproof and waterproof, so you do need a final layer on top. But because the fleece keeps you warm, there's no need for a heavy coat or anorak. Instead, just slip on an ultra-light 'shell' – waterproof and windproof, yet easily folding up into a neat package to be stored in a pocket or rucksack when the weather improves.

Birders are notoriously conservative, and it may be some time before they cast off their traditional anoraks in favour of the new materials. But you don't have to follow the herd – why not give the new approach a try? When everyone else is complaining about being too cold, or sweating under the burden of being overdressed, you'll be glad that you did!

Birding in hot climates brings its own set of problems. You may need to wear long trousers tucked into socks, and a long-sleeved shirt, to avoid mites and ticks. Sometimes, you can get away with shorts and a T-shirt, although if you do, then a high factor sun lotion is another essential, especially if you plan to stay out birding all day. Again, make sure that you go to a specialist outdoor clothing shop and get lightweight, hard-wearing items made out of a breathable material that will wick away moisture and leave you cool and comfortable. They may cost a little more than your usual leisure wear, but it's worth it – birding when you're uncomfortable is no fun!

2 IDENTIFYING BIRDS

When you see a bird, it is only natural to want
to put a name to it. Human beings are born with the
urge to categorise and catalogue the world around
them – to make sense of it by giving names – and this
is just as true with birds as with anything else. Indeed
this is an urge that has its roots in our ancestors'
need to know more about the world they
inhabited in order to survive. It should come as
no surprise to discover that most bird names
we use today are many centuries old, often
having their roots in Anglo-Saxon.

WHY IDENTIFY BIRDS?

Today's needs may not seem quite so urgent, but the desire to identify the birds you see certainly springs from that same primitive want. By doing so successfully, most birders gain an enormous amount of satisfaction.

However, putting the correct name to the bird you see is not an end in itself. Just as our ancestors would have used the correct identification of a bird in order to hunt and kill it for food, or domesticate it for its eggs and feathers, so by identifying a bird we open up a whole new world of understanding.

So don't fight your primeval urges: make an effort to name every bird you see (and just as importantly, hear!). It will accelerate the process of learning, give you a deeper insight into the daily lives of birds, and ultimately make you a better birder.

FIRST PRINCIPLES

Most birders, when faced with an unfamiliar bird, do one of four things. Some give up and move on to something else, taking the view that immature gulls, flying raptors, or 'little brown jobs', are simply impossible to identify correctly. Others use a little more initiative, and ask a companion or more experienced birder to tell them what they're looking at. A third category turn immediately to their field guide, searching until they have found the illustration that most closely matches the mystery bird.

All of these work up to a point, but they are short-term solutions, which will do little to help you when you next come across a similar problem. But there's a fourth option. Simply look at the bird properly. Make a clear mental picture, concentrating especially on unusual features, and if you can, by comparing it with similar species nearby. Then take brief, clear notes, once again focusing on key features which will help you identify the bird later.

Once you feel that you are truly familiar with the bird's appearance, begin the reference process, or seek advice from other birders. You'll still find that some individual birds prove difficult, perhaps even impossible to identify. But whether you succeed or fail, you'll have extended your store of knowledge, which will enable you to identify, with confidence, most birds you come across.

Most novice birders would find this Garden Warbler tricky to identify.

PROBABILITY THEORY

Once kept in cages by the Victorians for their song and stunning looks, Goldfinches are common British birds.

When you begin watching birds, almost every one you see appears to be new and unusual. Soon, however, you get used to the fact that there are 50 or so common species that make up 90% of the birds you see regularly; and another 50 species that constitute another 9%. Well under one in a hundred birds you come across is truly unfamiliar.

This is reflected in the rate at which you will accumulate new species on your 'life list'. After birding for a year or so you will probably have seen upwards of 120–150 species; after another year you should reach the 200 mark. After that it gets progressively more difficult to add more new birds, and unless you regularly go twitching, or visit far-flung parts of Britain in search of rare breeding birds, you may take a very long time to see 250 different species in this country.

So although that spanking new guide to the birds of Europe, with its 700 plus species, may appear daunting at first, you can more or less forget three-quarters of the birds it contains; instead concentrate on the 100 or so species you are likely to come across on a regular basis. As for the other 9,500 or so different kinds of bird in the world, they can wait a while!

IDENTIFICATION PROBLEMS AND PITFALLS

SAME SPECIES, DIFFERENT APPEARANCE

Now the bad news. There may only be 100 or so species to learn about, but each of them may present a whole range of identification problems. Take the humble House Sparrow, surely Britain's most familiar bird (albeit now a declining one).

Sparrows don't all look the same: like many species, including the Chaffinch, Mallard and Kestrel, they have distinctive male and female plumages – or to put it in technical language, are sexually dimorphic. Sexual dimorphism is not consistent amongst families: for example ducks show it, but geese and swans don't. Some birds of prey, a few warblers, most finches (but not all buntings), and various odd species such as the Blackbird show it; most others do not. The only way to know which species have different-looking males and females is to learn them one by one!

Many birds don't show sexual dimorphism, but they do have distinctive breeding and non-breeding plumages. For example, Black-headed Gulls undergo a twice-yearly moult from their breeding plumage (showing a brown – not black – hood) to their non-breeding one (with a brownish spot behind the ear). Just to make things even more confusing, young Black-headed Gulls go through a variety of plumage changes, too, and may appear quite different from the adults. This is where a good knowledge of structure is vital: an experienced birder can tell a Black-headed Gull apart from other gull species on its overall appearance and shape (*See* 'Jizz', p35).

Field guides sometimes create problems for the beginner by captioning these annual variations as 'summer' and 'winter' plumages. This is quite inaccurate, as many birds begin to moult immediately after breeding, adopting the so-called 'winter' plumage as early as July. Species such as the Great Crested Grebe may adopt their 'summer' dress as early as January, in preparation for the coming breeding season. For this reason, we prefer to refer to these different plumage states as 'breeding' and 'non-breeding' plumage.

Sexual dimorphism is very apparent in ducks. Males tend to be more brightly-coloured than females as shown here with the male and female Pochard.

The best way to learn the different plumage stages of each species is to observe them regularly during the course of a calendar year. Take careful notes of plumage changes, and remember that even within the same species, individual birds may change their appearance at different times, so you often see breeding and non-breeding plumages alongside each other in the same flock.

Some species, such as the larger gulls, go through a really complex set of moults before they reach adulthood. So a Herring Gull, for example, has as many as eight or ten distinct 'immature' plumages as well as its familiar adult garb. Some birders enjoy the challenge this poses, and spend hours critically examining young gulls on a feather-by-feather basis. Others can't be bothered, and go off and look at something else instead! But even if you don't have the patience of Job, it's still worth acquiring a working knowledge of gull plumages, so that when a rarer species such as a Mediterranean or Yellow-legged Gull turns up at your local reservoir you know how to identify it.

Gulls can be some of the hardest birds to identify because they take several years to reach adult plumage. Black-headed Gulls, illustrated above, show a variety of plumages: (from the top) first winter, adult in non-breeding plumage, first summer and adult in breeding plumage.

DIFFERENT SPECIES, SAME APPEARANCE

So that's the difficult stuff out of the way, right? Wrong! The real bugbear of most birders is what are termed 'confusion species': two different species which look very similar, if not virtually alike to the untrained eye.

Take the Chiffchaff and Willow Warbler. These two species of warbler have similar males and females, and show only minimal plumage variation through the seasons, so should be easy to identify. But they're not. Like other pairs of similar looking birds such as Willow and Marsh Tits, Chiffchaff and Willow Warbler are what are known as 'sibling species'. This means that they have recently evolved from a common ancestor, and as a result may show very similar traits. Indeed, Chiffchaff and Willow Warbler were only distinguished from each other just over two hundred years ago, when the pioneering ornithologist Gilbert White took a closer look at them – and most importantly, listened to their very distinctive songs.

Species with very similar appearance are also often called 'confusion species'. Although these are often related to one another, that is not always the case. For example, Black Kite and Marsh Harrier are more likely to be confused with each other

The Chiffchaff (above) is usually duller-looking than the Willow Warbler (left). When in doubt, look for the darker legs on the Chiffchaff.

than with more closely related species such as Red Kite and Hen Harrier. In some cases, the similarity is entirely superficial: when you first see a Cuckoo fly past, your first reaction will probably be to assume it is a falcon or hawk, due to its very similar appearance in flight.

Other groups of birds are easy to identify in most plumages, and at most times of year – but cause identification headaches at other times. The best example of this is the so-called 'eclipse plumage' of ducks such as the Mallard, Gadwall and Shoveler, in which the males moult into a drab plumage quite different from their fine-looking breeding garb. In breeding plumage, the Ruff is one of the most obvious of all waders. Yet once it has moulted into its non-breeding dress, it can be a real headache to identify, particularly as the large males and small females often appear to be two entirely different species.

Some species are nearly always seen in Britain in their drab, non-breeding plumage. The breeding male Common Rosefinch is resplendent in scarlet, but autumn juveniles look like a thin,

The Willow Tit (above) seems to have a stockier neck than the very similar Marsh Tit (left). It also shows a pale patch on the wing. However, the easiest way to tell these birds apart is by their call.

Moulting male Mallards can be hard to identify: this plumage is known as 'eclipse'.

streaky sparrow. Grebes and divers in non-breeding plumage are far harder to identify than during the breeding season.

For other confusion species, the problem is not that of plumage detail, but the conditions under which they are usually seen. Given good views, Cory's and Great Shearwaters are quite easy to tell apart, both on plumage detail and jizz. But when you're watching them in driving rain, at a distance of a mile or more, then you'll usually have to put them down simply as 'large shearwater species'.

In contrast, this pair of Mallards in breeding plumage can easily be identified.

FAMILY RESEMBLANCES

What if you don't even know which family the bird belongs to? That little bird crawling around a ploughed field could be a lark or a pipit, a finch or a bunting – so where do you start? Again, it's important to learn the key features that distinguish one group of birds from another: for example, all pipits have a longish, slender bill for feeding on insects, while finches and buntings have a stout bill for eating seeds.

Another problem is the equivalent of what my old French teacher used to call 'faux amis': words that look like one thing but mean another. Birds have their equivalents: for example, not every bird that swims on fresh water is a duck: it might be a Coot or Moorhen, diver or grebe, or even a gull! Again, get used to the distinguishing features for whole families and you'll soon find things get easier. As always with bird identification, there's no substitute for a combination of observation and experience.

Hawfinches have stout bills for eating seeds.

Meadow Pipits have fine thin bills for catching insects.

Even though a juvenile Greenfinch isn't green, its bill shape tells you that it is a finch.

AGEING BIRDS

You may feel you've got to grips with the familiar species, when something a bit different turns up in the garden. It's shaped like a Robin, it behaves like a Robin, but there's one big difference: no orange breast. Instead, it's a fairly nondescript buffish-brown, with paler markings on the breast and back.

In fact it is a Robin – a young bird hatched this year. This stage, the first covering of feathers replacing the down of the new-born chick, is known as juvenile plumage. Later in the year, if it's lucky enough to survive the perils of cats and other garden hazards, it will undergo its first moult. In the case of the Robin and most other songbirds, it will adopt an adult plumage in the autumn after hatching.

The juvenile Robin lacks the stunning red breast of the adult.

With its bluish-black plumage and red and yellow bill, the adult Moorhen is a handsome bird.

Late summer can be a confusing time, as your garden or local park may be full of juvenile birds. In most cases, a little patience will enable you to identify which species they belong to; and if you can't do so, you can always wait until the parents show up!

As autumn approaches, you may want to venture farther afield to take a close look at waders. Some, especially the earlier migrants, will be adult birds, usually sporting a rather unkempt appearance as they moult out of their bright breeding plumage into drab winter dress. But from late August onwards, the majority will be juveniles, their fresh, clean appearance quite different from the worn feathers of the adults.

In contrast, the juvenile Moorhen is a dull colour and may cause confusion at first sight.

As you become more confident at pinpointing the plumage of a particular bird, and therefore its age, the identification of this tricky group of birds becomes much easier. As always, the best way to learn is by trial and error. So next time you're out in the field, try to go further than simply identifying the species, and see if you can work out the bird's age, too.

OUT OF CONTEXT BIRDS

It's an autumn day, and you're birding along the coast. Suddenly, you catch sight of a small, brownish-green bird on the shingle beach in front of you. You focus your binoculars, and to your surprise, it looks like a small warbler. A closer look reveals dark legs, short wings and dull, poorly-marked supercilium – it's a Chiffchaff. But it can't be – after all, the field guides say that this species lives in woodland or scrub. So what could it possibly be doing on a beach? In fact, your initial identification was correct: it is a Chiffchaff. On migration, birds can turn up in the most unexpected places, a long way from their typical breeding habitat. For the new birdwatcher this can be confusing, and often lead to errors in identification.

When I started watching birds, every pipit I saw near the sea was a 'Rock Pipit'. I now know that Meadow Pipits frequently live on the coast, and in some places are more likely to be encountered there than their scarcer relative. Nor is the problem confined to beginners. Every autumn experienced birdwatchers on the Isles of Scilly misidentify common-or-garden warblers as much rarer species, simply because the bird is in an unfamiliar context, away from its usual habitat.

So what should you do when you come across one of these 'out-of-context' birds? First, forget any preconceptions about habitat – a migrant can turn up almost anywhere. Second, try to judge the bird's size – though this can be difficult with a lone bird, when familiar 'landmarks' are absent. Finally, note down details of plumage and behaviour.

Beware of different light conditions: a bird you've seen many times in its typical woodland habitat may appear quite different when in full sunlight, against an unusual background. Above all, avoid making assumptions. Try to focus on the bird itself, rather than the context in which you find it. What species does it look like to you? Have you seen it before, in a different habitat? Memory is an underrated tool in bird identification, so use it to the full. You won't be able to identify every out-of-context bird you see, but it's always worth having a try.

On migration, birds can turn up anywhere! This Reed Warbler landed on a passenger's hat during a boat journey.

top tip

USE A FIELD GUIDE

Once you've taken field notes, it's time to do some detective work. And every good detective needs help: in this case, from a field guide. But don't rely on them too much: always look at the bird first, then use the field guide to help you check key identification features.

Ruddy Shelducks are frequently seen in Britain. However, it is thought that none are truly wild birds, but escapes from captivity or wanderers from feral populations on the Continent.

Red-breasted and Snow Geese are often kept in wildfowl collections, but at least some of the birds seen in Britain are thought to be wild.

Blackbirds and Ring Ouzels are not always easy to tell apart: this Blackbird is partially albino, and the white feathering can cause confusion with its scarcer relative.

ESCAPES

October is the month when thousands of birdwatchers follow the birds to migration watchpoints from one end of the British Isles to the other, in search of rare vagrants from the four corners of the globe. But how can they be sure that the bird they are watching really has flown hundreds of miles from Siberia or North America, and not just travelled from the nearest cage or aviary? If birders were brutally honest, they would have to admit that in many cases they can't be absolutely sure that this sought-after vagrant isn't really an escape. Indeed, evidence shows that on many occasions the bird is undoubtedly not a genuine vagrant.

It has been suggested that the fact that so many alleged 'escapes' turn up in May and October in places like Scilly and Shetland is an argument in favour of a wild origin. Unfortunately this shows a lack of understanding both of bird behaviour and basic statistics. Escaped birds are likely to revert to their original instincts, which will often include an urge to migrate in spring and autumn. Also, the number of experienced observers at these 'hotspots' means that any passing bird will be carefully scrutinised, and most likely identified; whereas if the bird hangs around in a less well-watched part of the country it will probably die before it encounters a birdwatcher.

A few birders are prepared to face up to the unpalatable truth that many of the species generally regarded as genuine vagrants may contain a high proportion of escapes. In the end, most will continue to decide for themselves which individuals and which species they consider to be escapes, and which they can safely tick. But rest assured, while birds are kept in captivity, this controversy will doubtless continue.

FREAKS AND ODDBALLS

Then there are the oddballs: birds that show unusual or freak plumages, such as an albino blackbird, which will appear all white instead of black. These are rare, but when they do turn up can be very confusing. Other birds may show a patch of white in the wing or on the head; or may have a deformed bill, or have lost all their tail-feathers to a predator; or may simply be so sick that they look nothing like a healthy member of the species. Just be aware that these freaks and oddballs do occur, so when you see something that looks like nothing you've ever seen before, don't automatically jump to the conclusion that it must be a very rare bird!

APPROACHES TO IDENTIFICATION

JIZZ VS THE FEATHER-BY FEATHER APPROACH

'Jizz' is one of those strange pieces of birdwatcher's slang which can be baffling if you haven't come across it before. It refers to the overall 'feel' of a bird, which picks it out as a particular species even if you can't see all – or indeed any – of the plumage details.

Note the differences in flight between the Buzzard (top) and the Osprey (above). The Buzzard's wings are broader and more rounded, while the Osprey has long, kinked wings.

You may have to rely on jizz alone when a bird is distant. The overall shape and long, decurved bill identifies this bird as a Curlew.

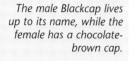

The male Blackcap lives up to its name, while the female has a chocolate-brown cap.

Jizz is one of the best ways to identify raptors in flight: the hovering of the Kestrel (above), and the plunge-diving behaviour of the Osprey (below) are diagnostic.

You know from experience that you can often identify a familiar species by its general appearance or silhouette. Think of a hovering Kestrel or the rear view of a Robin, which will immediately tell you the bird's identity. Just as you can often spot a familiar face in a crowd of people, so the combination of shape and movement means it can only be that species. The origins of the word are puzzling. Some say it's World War Two US Air Force slang for the ability to identify a distant aircraft by its 'general image and shape', or 'g.i.s.', but others have pointed out that the pioneering British ornithologist T.A. Coward used the word back in the 1920s.

The advantage of jizz is that it can work given poor views. It does depend, however, on being very familiar with the species concerned, in as many different circumstances as possible. It's also worth thinking about why a particular bird can be identified by its jizz, and how other, closely-related species might appear different.

A different technique is characterised by the 'New Approach to Identification', devised by Killian Mullarney and the late Peter Grant. Grant and Mullarney maintained that while jizz is undoubtedly useful, it shouldn't be relied on, and there is no substitute for a detailed description of the bird's plumage, using a thorough knowledge of bird topography (*see* opposite).

No one would doubt that jizz has its drawbacks. Birds sometimes behave very differently from the way you'd expect: they fluff out their feathers against the cold, use an unusual feeding technique, or appear in an unfamiliar habitat. Relying on jizz alone can lead to embarrassing mistakes, or to overlooking something rare simply because it was behaving like its commoner relative.

Fortunately you don't have to choose between the two techniques. Jizz is always a very useful way of picking out something unusual, especially when you're scanning through a mixed flock, such as waders or ducks. But once you've latched onto the bird, then take detailed notes of specific plumage details and behaviour to clinch the identification.

BIRD TOPOGRAPHY

Topography, as its name suggests, is basically the external 'map' of a bird's plumage and bare parts – i.e. the feathers, bill, legs and feet. It is used both by scientists and by ordinary birdwatchers, to help identify or age a particular bird.

Although many species of birds look superficially similar, and indeed some may only be fully identifiable in the hand, there are always subtle differences between species if you look long and hard enough.

On a more basic level, learning the topography of bird plumages can enable you to distinguish between similar species. Indeed, if you talk about 'wingbars' and 'head-pattern' you are already well on the way to learning bird topography.

Cuckoo

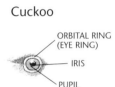

Redwing

Female Reed Bunting

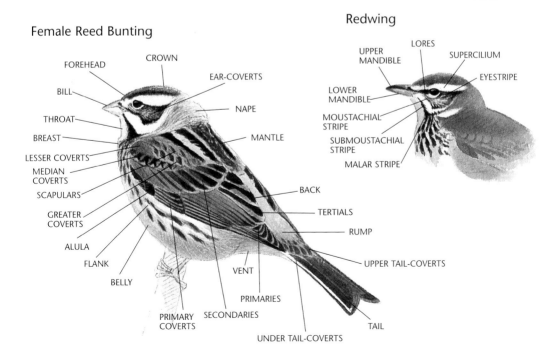

The problem with such general terms, however, is that they can be ambiguous, and may be little or no use when it comes to really tricky species such as stints or unusual warblers. When it comes to confusion species like these, there really is no substitute for mastering the finer details of bird topography. Terms such as 'median coverts', 'supercilium' and 'culmen' may at first seem obscure and hard to learn, but with a little persistence, and practice in the field, they will open a new dimension to your birding.

Blackcaps often sing in deep foliage, so knowing their song is vital if you want to identify them in spring.

LEARNING BIRD SONGS

When it comes to bird identification, it's easy to concentrate on the appearance of a bird. This is all fine and dandy until you come across those species that either look alike, or spend their time hidden from view in trees or bushes. That's when a thorough knowledge of birdsong comes into its own.

Many birders find identifying birds by song alone difficult. There are, however, a number of ways in which you can ease the pain of learning. The first is to use mnemonics: little reminders that help you remember a particular species' call or song. A friend of mine uses familiar names to remember bird calls – for example, 'Chiswick' is Pied Wagtail! The song of the Yellowhammer has often been described as saying 'a-little-bit-of-bread-and-no-cheeese', while the Chaffinch always sounds to me like a fast-bowling cricketer running up to deliver!

Perhaps an easier way is to take advantage of new technology, and use a portable tape recorder or compact disc player. There are all kinds of birdsong recordings on the market, from a four-volume guide to almost 400 European species, to ones featuring specific families like larks, nightingales or warblers. There are also 'teach yourself' tapes which cover a particular group such as 'woodland birds', and guide you painlessly through the process of learning songs and calls.

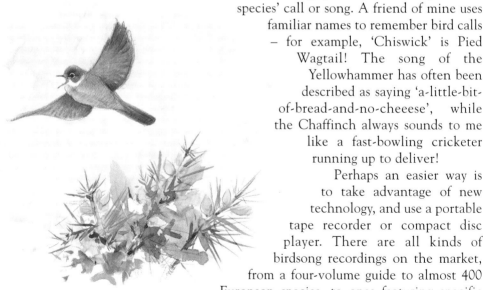

Whitethroats are more obliging, and often launch themselves into the air while singing in their 'parachuting display'.

Whether or not you prefer tapes or CDs is a matter of personal choice. Tapes are cheaper, and can easily be taken in to the field, but the quality isn't so good, and they don't have the random access facility of CDs. CDs are certainly better for use at home: they sound brilliant, being virtually hiss-free, and give almost instant, random access to any track, allowing you to improve your knowledge by testing yourself. Some people now put bird songs onto minidisc, which has the advantage of portability and random access.

The male Reed Bunting has a hesitant but distinctive song, which always sounds to me like someone saying 'One... two... testing...'

One of the best times of the year to learn how to identify birds by their song is early spring. For our resident breeders such as tits and thrushes, the courtship ritual is in full swing, and the male birds are singing to defend a territory and win a mate. From a practical point of view, it's also a lot easier to catch sight of singing birds before the trees come into bud, and it helps your confidence no end if you can clinch your identification by actually seeing the bird as it sings.

Later in the spring, when the summer visitors begin to return, you can extend your knowledge by getting to grips with groups like warblers and flycatchers. By the end of the breeding season, when it's all gone quiet, you should have a pretty good grounding in identifying birds by song. Just make sure you keep practising with the tapes or CDs during the autumn and winter, or by the following spring you'll have forgotten it all again!

GETTING TO GRIPS WITH CALLS

To those of us without musical knowledge or training, learning birdsong can be a difficult chore. But at least songs give you something to commit to memory – a tune, a descent of the scale, or perhaps a memorable flourish at the end. In contrast, bird calls are frequently just a monosyllabic 'tweet' – the aural equivalent of the 'little brown job'. Given this, and the

top tip

JOIN AN ORGANIZATION OR TWO

Birdwatching is all about co-operative activity: so join your local Wildlife Trust and/or your local bird club. You'll meet like-minded people and be able to put something back to help the birds.

inadequacy of human language to describe bird sounds, is it any wonder that many birders give up in despair?

But think again. You can learn bird calls, and late autumn and winter is the ideal time of year to do so. Not only are many birds becoming active in search of food, but because there is little or no foliage on the trees, you can confirm your judgement by seeing the bird as well. The first thing to remember is that birds call for a whole variety of reasons, so each species may have a very varied repertoire of calls. Take the Blackbird. The most familiar and easy-to-memorise call is the repetitive, jangling alarm, usually heard as the bird crashes away from you through the undergrowth. One author described seven different

Given good views, the Sedge Warbler is easy to identify, but on a windy day you may need to rely on its song to tell it apart from the Reed Warbler.

A mixed flock of Blue Tits, Goldcrests and a Coal Tit: these birds will utter contact calls to stay in touch with each other while travelling through the foliage.

The Starling is well-known as an accomplished mimic, able to imitate other birds, car alarms and even mobile phones!

kinds of calls for the Blackbird, for purposes ranging from mild alarm to distress, as well as a low-pitched contact call made by migrating birds.

Perhaps the greatest variety of different calls can be found in the tit family. However familiar you are with the species, a Great Tit can always surprise you with something new! But it's well worth getting to know the calls of the commoner species, enabling you to pick up that unfamiliar note which may prove to be a Marsh or Willow Tit.

One way to learn bird calls is to concentrate on three different aspects: tone, rhythm and pitch. Judging pitch of a lone bird call can be difficult unless you have a musical ear, so try to compare it with a familiar sound if you can. Rhythm is easier to judge, but with so many bird calls being monosyllabic it has its limitations.

Tone is perhaps the most subjective category of all. Everyone has their own personal reaction to a sound, with the words 'fluty', 'thin' and 'reedy' meaning slightly different things to different people. But with practice and persistence, you will be able to use these techniques to develop your own aural memory, opening up a whole new world of knowledge and understanding.

top tip

FEED YOUR GARDEN BIRDS

When you begin birding, it can be difficult to get good views of birds. So if the birds won't let you get near them, why not persuade them to come to you, by setting up your very own feeding station.

BIRDS IN FLIGHT

Crows can be difficult to tell apart in flight: look out for the narrower wings of the Rook (right) compared with the Carrion Crow (centre); and the wedge-shaped tail and larger size of the Raven (left).

Mastering the basics of bird identification is never an easy task; indeed it could be argued that not even the greatest field experts ever become totally confident in their ability to put a firm identity to every bird they see. As a beginner, one of the hardest aspects of identification is dealing with birds in flight, for several reasons.

The two 'winter thrushes', Redwing and Fieldfare, have different flight silhouettes: the Redwings (below) appear small and compact, while the Fieldfare (right) has a long tail and pot belly!

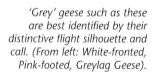

First, birds in flight are often flying away from the observer. So not only are you trying to identify the individual from a rear view, but you only have a minute or so before the bird is out of sight! Second, specific plumage features are often difficult to see on a moving bird; and even if you do think you've seen them, there's always a chance that a trick of the light was responsible.

Finally, flying birds are often viewed from unusual angles, not just from behind, but often below, especially in the case of geese,

'Grey' geese such as these are best identified by their distinctive flight silhouette and call. (From left: White-fronted, Pink-footed, Greylag Geese).

Sparrowhawk (female, far left and male, centre top) and Kestrel (female, left and male, above) are not always easy to tell apart in flight: look out for the long, pointed wings of the Kestrel and the more rounded wings of the Sparrowhawk.

raptors and other high-flying species. Indeed, birds of prey, like buzzards, hawks and eagles are so often seen in flight that most field guides concentrate primarily on this aspect of raptor identification; focusing on aspects such as wing-shape and head and tail projection, as well as the specific plumage details, which in any case are sometimes so variable that they don't allow you to assign the bird to a particular species.

Flight silhouettes are a particular problem, as the same species may appear very different, depending on the flight method it is using at the time of viewing. For instance, a Sparrowhawk may soar on relatively open wings, showing the characteristic 'T-shaped' silhouette; or it may stoop and dive on closed wings. Equally a Kestrel may hover obligingly above your head, or fly past on quite broad-looking wings, sometimes even suggesting the shape and jizz of a Sparrowhawk.

Song and Mistle Thrushes can be told apart by size, colour and overall 'jizz': Song Thrush (above) is smaller and more compact, with warmer plumage tones.

In flight Linnets show the familiar finch features – the long wings and forked tail.

Seabirds are even worse. Beware of identification guides which point confidently to a particular style of flight for birds like the rarer shearwaters, skuas and petrels. In 'normal' conditions they may well conform to this expected form of behaviour, but in unusually strong winds or calm weather they may act quite differently to how you expect.

Little Gull (left) and Common, Arctic and Sandwich Terns can be tricky to identify in flight, especially in autumn.

Little Gull Common Tern Arctic Tern Sandwich Tern

As always, the only way to be sure of what you're looking at is by getting to know each species thoroughly, and in as many different light and weather conditions as possible. Only then will you be able to confidently identify difficult species in flight. Even then, you should always be prepared to put some birds down as 'identification not proven'..

Green Woodpeckers have a distinctive flight, their long undulating glides are broken by short bursts of wingbeats.

In flight both male and female Chaffinches show double white wing bars, plus white outer tail feathers.

Redshanks get their name from their red legs or 'shanks'. Even juvenile birds (right) have the distinctive red legs.

LEARNING THE HARD WAY...

A friend of mine, Derek (not his real name) took up birding relatively late in life, after he had developed a successful career in business. He regarded his hobby as a kind of trial by combat, and found his inability to identify every single bird he saw very frustrating. The result? He never really enjoyed watching birds. You won't be surprised to hear that he soon gave it up, and took up some other, more controllable hobby.

His friend Mike took a more pragmatic approach. Confronted with a mixed group of waders, he focused on a single bird. He watched it for a while, and made a few notes. Then he looked at his field guide, then back at the bird. Finally, having satisfied himself, he gave his verdict: Spotted Redshank. What's more, he was right. Unlike Derek, Mike didn't feel that if he couldn't identify every single bird, he had failed the test. Nevertheless, he was far happier to have identified the Spotted Redshank than having it pointed out for him by a more experienced birder. Sure, his approach was harder work – but it paid off in the end.

In its handsome black breeding plumage (left) the Spotted Redshank is unmistakable; but outside the breeding season (above) it may be confused with the Redshank. Look out for the longer bill and plainer grey-brown plumage.

45

It's a bit like learning a foreign language. When you're a child, it's easy; but as an adult, it's a chore. Those of us who started birding at an early age are lucky: we made our really major identification errors when it didn't really matter. It's OK for a twelve-year-old to misidentify a Shelduck as an Avocet (as I did!) – but for an adult to make the same mistake is embarrassing, especially if you're in a packed hide at Minsmere.

This is a pity, because making mistakes is a key part of learning to identify birds: if

At first sight this female Reed Bunting looks like a typical 'little brown job', but given close views its head pattern is quite distinctive.

you never take a risk, you'll never learn. Take what birdwatchers call 'little brown jobs'. You can ignore them, and just pretend they're all sparrows. Or you can find out if they're something different.

I once pointed out a couple of female Reed Buntings to a novice birdwatcher. Her first reaction was dismissive: 'Oh, I never bother with those, they're too difficult.' But with a little encouragement she began to work out the key identification points for herself. Now if she sees a 'little brown job', perhaps she'll have the confidence to try to identify it on her own.

So next time you come up against a bird you can't put a name to, stop, take a deep breath, and start working out why it looks different. You may not solve the puzzle the first, or even second time, but when you do, you'll discover for yourself why it's worth persevering with bird identification.

The female House Sparrow doesn't have white in the wing.

The female Chaffinch and Sparrow look very similar; an easy way to quick identification is to look for the white in the wing on the Chaffinch.

...AND THE EASY WAY

So how can you make bird identification easier? Ultimately there is no substitute for experience – the more you see, the more you know, and the more confident you will get. But there is something you can do during the long, dark winter nights at home, to help when you're next out in the field.

Most groups or families of birds have particular distinguishing features that are key factors when it comes to telling similar species apart. With waders, length and shape of bill can be critical; with gulls, the wing-pattern is important. The better you know the key identification points, the more chance you will have of identifying an unfamiliar species. For example, let's assume you've come across a strange female duck. You may only have a limited time to take notes before it flies away – so it's vital that you concentrate on the right things. Forget about bill and leg colour – the key point is usually the colour of the speculum (that little patch of colour on the closed wing).

With warblers, on the other hand, things like leg colour, relative length of the wing and tail, or size and shape of the supercilium may be more important. Some species are best told apart by their call or song, like Willow Warbler and Chiffchaff; although given good views they can also be told apart by subtle differences in structure and plumage, such as the Chiffchaff's shorter wings and darker legs.

Learning these key ID points isn't easy: it takes a combination of a good memory, practice in the field, and experience. But if you know what to look for, you'll avoid wasting time on irrelevant details, and stand a better chance of clinching the correct identification.

A quick way to tell the above Whimbrel from a Curlew is by the obvious white head stripes on the Whimbrel.

The long bill and the stocky body of the Snipe helps identification from a distance.

Oystercatchers cannot be confused with any other wader in the UK. Non-breeding birds have a white chinstrap.

SIZE-ILLUSION

When you see an unfamiliar bird for the first time, you begin the process of working out its identity. The first step is often to judge the bird's size, usually by comparing it with a more familiar, related species. So a strange-looking wader may be described as 'a little larger than a Dunlin', or 'smaller than a Knot'; while a small warbler may be 'bulkier than a Chiffchaff'.

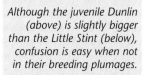

Or you may forgo a direct comparison, and try to estimate the actual length of the bird instead – even down to the nearest inch or centimetre. Many a description of an unfamiliar rare bird has begun with the words 'About 18 cm long'. But however you choose to estimate the size of a bird, chances are you'll be wrong. You won't be miles out – after all, a smallish wader is likely to be somewhere between 14 and 22 cm long – but nevertheless your estimate is likely to be far from accurate.

Stop and think about it for a moment. If someone held up a children's toy or a paperback book, would you be confident of knowing its exact length? You might make a reasonable guess, but you'd still probably be around 10% to 20% out. So why do you assume you can estimate the size of a lone bird any better?

Whether or not you realise it, when you judge the size of any bird you're making a series of assumptions about its identity. It looks like a Dunlin, so it must be between 16 and 20 cm long. It flies like a Kestrel, so it must have a wingspan of about 70 cm.

Making these assumptions can lead to major mistakes. I've seen a Merlin (25–30 cm long) misidentified as a Peregrine (40–50 cm) – and vice versa! I've caught sight of a distant Goshawk through a telescope, and for a moment thought the long, narrow wings belonged to a Kestrel. I've seen a faraway, female Common Scoter misidentified as both Smew and Ruddy Duck, just because everyone assumed it was a small duck rather than a large one. All these mistakes occurred when the observers were faced with a lone bird, without the advantage of comparison with more familiar species. But beware – direct comparison between two individual birds can be just as misleading, due to a bizarre phenomenon known as size-illusion.

Size-illusion was first noticed by the late Peter Grant, when high-powered telescopes first became popular during the 1980s. While viewing two Little Stints through a scope, Grant noticed

Although the juvenile Dunlin (above) is slightly bigger than the Little Stint (below), confusion is easy when not in their breeding plumages.

Goshawks are rare birds in the UK, but female Sparrowhawks are often mistaken for these birds due to their large size.

that the more distant bird appeared to be bigger. But when the two birds swapped their position, the other bird, now behind its companion, looked bigger. Grant realised that this might lead an incautious or inexperienced observer to assume that the rear bird was the slightly larger, and much rarer, Semipalmated Sandpiper.

After consulting optical experts, Grant discovered the reason for this apparent anomaly. When you view two similar-sized birds with the naked eye, one behind the other, your brain compensates for the apparent difference in size. So you know that despite appearing smaller, the more distant bird is in fact the same size as the one in the foreground.

Female ducks can be an identification nightmare; you may need careful observation and patience to identify this female Ruddy Duck.

But when you look through high-powered optical aids, there is a foreshortening effect, which makes both birds appear much closer than they actually are. This has the result of making the relative distance between the two birds appear greater than in reality. Your brain compensates as if you were using your naked eye, and thus the bird behind looks appreciably bigger than its companion.

Female Common Scoter. The pale cheeks of other female diving ducks can lead to confusion.

If this sounds confusing, go out in the field and try it – you'll be amazed at the results. And next time you're trying to work out a bird's size, beware. Remember the twin perils of size-illusion, and plain mistaken identity, and never make assumptions!

TO SUM UP

So just to recap: some species show two or more different plumages, depending on the time of year, or whether you are looking at a male, female or young bird. Others don't show much variety, but appear confusingly similar to another closely-related species, or even to another quite different bird.

Some can look quite different when seen out of context, for example on migration; while others can show some kind of plumage mutation such as albinism, making them appear very different from the norm.

Some birds don't show themselves at all, and only sing or call from dense foliage. Others fly high, or against the sun, or rapidly away from you.

Some birds look similar even though they are separate species, like this male and female Tufted Duck (right – male at bottom) and Scaup (below – male at bottom)

The male and female Twite are very similar, but an experienced birder will notice the male has a pale pink rump during the breeding season.

Male Pied Flycatchers, as their name suggests, have a distinctive black-and-white plumage, while females are a much duller brown.

Some aren't 'real' birds at all, but have just hopped out of a nearby cage or aviary, while others are perfectly normal in every way, but because of the phenomenon of size-illusion they appear bigger or smaller than the bird next door.

Confused? So you should be! Let's face it, if every bird was so easy to identify that you could get it right every time, half the fun of birding would be lost. Much of the enjoyment gained when watching birds is down to the fact that each bird presents a new identification challenge.

It is this that makes birdwatching such a wonderful mixture of sport, aesthetics and hunting (and not at all like trainspotting!). Every bird should invite close scrutiny, however sure you think you are of the species, and not even the experienced birder can afford to drop their guard, for you never quite know what will turn up next!

top tip

SUBSCRIBE TO ONE OR TWO BIRDING MAGAZINES

There are several monthly magazines available packed with advice and information, on everything from local patchwork to birding abroad – guaranteed to help you make the most of your new interest. Some are available at high street newsagents, others on subscription.

3 FIELDCRAFT

The term 'fieldcraft' is a complex one,
encompassing the skills, ability and experience
you will need to develop to make the most of your
birding. In essence, it comes down to a heightened
awareness: both of the habits and behaviour of the
birds themselves, and the ability to develop self-
awareness – to see yourself as the birds see you.
This may take years – indeed a lifetime –
to learn, but there are some basic lessons
you can begin to learn straight away, which
will help you make the most of
your birding.

BEING AWARE

Fieldcraft begins the moment you step out into the 'field' – anywhere you might be watching birds. Your senses must be heightened, ready to notice the slightest movement, register the faintest sound, and notice anything out of the ordinary. For only by taking in and interpreting every piece of evidence will you be able to develop your skills as a birder.

The art of fieldcraft involves the way you dress, the way you walk, the way you look and listen, indeed every way you behave. In its wider sense it also means knowledge: of the best places to go to watch birds, which birds are found in which habitat, the best time of day and the best time of year to see particular birds. By developing skills that eventually become part of your instinct, you'll find that wherever you go in the world you can enjoy watching birds.

Fieldcraft is not something you can pick up in a day, or even a year. It is a lifelong learning process, which even the most experienced and expert birders continue to develop. Just like learning a language, it involves progressing from 'getting by', to fluency, via an understanding of the subtle nuances that make the difference between a good experience, and a great one.

FIELDCRAFT BEGINS AT HOME

You can begin developing your fieldcraft skills anywhere, even at home. Stand in your garden, and look around you. At first, there may be very little evidence of birds at all; but then you notice a movement out of the corner of your eye; hear a thin 'seep' or 'tic' call; or notice a flock of birds flying in the far distance.

Fieldcraft is all about blending in with the surrounding habitat and trying to sense the birds' movements and behaviour.

Try to imagine that this is the very first time you have ever come across birds; register everything that will help you track down and identify them. What is it about that flying bird that makes it a gull: is it the shape and size, structure, or something not related to appearance, such as the fact that it is flying together with a flock of similar birds? Where are they going? Do they only pass this way occasionally, or every day at a regular time? Would they still be here at a different time of year?

Birds follow patterns of behaviour, and the more you observe them the quicker you will become familiar with these. They also

respond to your presence in a particular way: some, like pigeons and doves, will flee the moment they see you; others, like the Robin, may be so tame that they will eventually come to your hand to feed. It's always best to keep movement to a minimum, and dress in muted colours. But more than this, you should try to blend in with the wider environment, to become part of it, so that the birds eventually ignore your presence and get on with whatever they were doing before you arrived.

Of course, birds behave differently under different circumstances. My old local patch was the haunt of dog-walkers and joggers galore, and as a result the birds were extremely tame and approachable. Even shy species such as Jays would give great views, while less flighty ones like grebes and ducks came incredibly close. At another location, the same species might be very wary – it all depends on the particular factors involved.

Usually shy and wary, Jays may allow very close approach in places where they have got used to people, such as town parks.

If in doubt, assume that most birds will fly away when they see or hear you, and behave accordingly!

WALKING AND WAITING

Some birders prefer to go and find the birds – the 'leggers'.

A legendary Scottish ornithologist, Desmond Nethersole-Thompson, once divided birders into two camps: 'arsers' and 'leggers'. Leggers spend their time rushing around from one place to another, with the aim of covering as much ground as possible. Arsers, as their name suggests, prefer a more leisurely approach, spending long periods of time sitting still and waiting for the birds to come to them.

Of course both strategies have their uses. The more habitats you cover, the more birds you are likely to see, especially in spring and autumn, when migrating birds may be passing rapidly through an area. On the other hand, rushing about inevitably leads to missing out on some of the more skulking species, which may require a bit more patience to get to grips with.

While other birders prefer to sit and wait for the birds to come to them – the 'arsers'.

Twitchers know this well – despite their public image, they often spend long periods of time waiting for their target bird to appear. In the meantime, they may get unexpected views of something else. While waiting for the appearance of a Spotted Crake a few years ago I had great views of another shy species, the Water Rail, several of which emerged onto small patches of mud at the base of a reedbed.

Sitting in one place also enables you to get better views than if you move about a lot. Birds react to movement, so if you stay still and try to blend in with the landscape you'll be amazed at how closely they will approach. This particularly applies to tired migrants or birds in cold winter weather, when they have more on their minds than being disturbed by humans.

On the whole, most birders spend rather too much time on the move. Next time you're out in the field try the alternative approach – you'll be amazed by the results!

To get a good view of a Water Rail you'll need to be prepared to wait a while.

THE INVISIBLE BIRD

What's the most frustrating thing about birding? For most people, it's 'missing' a bird – being unable to get your binoculars onto an individual that everyone else can see. This is a particular problem with small, skulking species such as warblers, which tend to flit from branch to branch of a bush or tree, making them very hard to pin down.

At times you can almost believe the bird is a figment of your companions' imagination. You can hear their exclamations of delight, or their discussions of the bird's important plumage features, and you're dying to join in – but you still can't see the blasted thing!

So what should you do? Well, first, don't panic. Take a deep breath, and try to work out where they're looking. Remember, to them it's obvious where the bird is, and their directions are likely to be annoyingly vague. Advice like, 'it's in that bush over there...' and 'just behind that branch...' aren't really very useful. You could try standing directly behind them, and looking at

Pointing out a bird to someone else can take practice!

This Wood Warbler is doing a fine impression of a leaf, making it difficult to see!

where their binoculars are pointing. Chances are, however, that you'll just get a view of the back of someone's head.

So have a go at finding the bird for yourself. Start without the binoculars, and try to judge the general direction. Is it high or low? To the left, right or straight ahead? Most importantly, how far away is it? I've lost count of the number of times I finally caught sight of a target bird, only to discover it was far closer than I was originally looking. Watch for movement – not always easy on a windy day, when every waving leaf looks like a small warbler.

Then, when you've got the bird with your naked eye, lift your binoculars quickly but carefully, making sure you're pointing them as close to the movement as you can. Turn the focus wheel back and forth, and with luck, the bird will miraculously appear in your field of view.

Finally, be realistic. You'll never get a good view of every bird, however hard you try. Some birds, unfortunately, will always remain invisible – the birdwatcher's equivalent of the one that got away.

Goldcrests are small and fast-moving, so can be difficult to locate.

CLOCKING ON

Here's a quick tip for giving directions on finding a bird to another birdwatcher. Assume that the direction you're facing is the top of a clock face: 12 o'clock. Therefore your field of view ranges from 9 o'clock on the far left, to 3 o'clock on the far right. So if the bird is dead ahead, you can call out 'Marsh Harrier, flying right at 12 o'clock'. If it has just come into view on the right of your field of vision, it's 'flying left at 2 o'clock'.

This system is especially useful in two situations: seawatching and hides. For seawatchers, the lack of landmarks means that the clock system is invaluable in pinpointing the general direction of a passing bird. In a hide, it means that everyone can get a quicker view of a bird.

But beware. You all have to be looking the same way for the clock system to work. Also, not everyone grasps the system, and it's easy to make mistakes. The commonest problem is 'clock reversal', in which 10 o'clock is confused with 2 o'clock, or vice versa. And some people never get the hang of it, such as the novice birder who yelled confidently 'Avocet at twenty past six!' Still, no one's perfect.

LOOKING AND LISTENING: *WINTER*

A wood in winter can seem almost entirely devoid of birds, particularly on a cold afternoon when the light is failing and your mind and body are telling you to go home to the warm. But don't give up. The birds haven't gone missing – they're just playing hard to get.

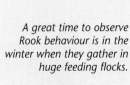

A great time to observe Rook behaviour is in the winter when they gather in huge feeding flocks.

In winter, birds often come together in a flock to forage for food. So they aren't evenly spread throughout the whole habitat, as they tend to be during the breeding season, but are concentrated in one or two places – usually where the food

supply is most abundant. At times, discovering a flock of birds in a winter woodland is a bit like looking for the proverbial needle in a very large haystack. So how do you find them?

The answer is simple: use your senses. In this case, hearing is more important than sight, as individual birds within a flock generally give out a series of brief sounds as they go along. These are known as 'contact calls', and their purpose is to keep the bird in touch with the rest of the flock, and to guide others to sources of food.

The commonest species found in a woodland flock are usually tits, with Blue and Great Tits generally the most vocal. Listen for the scolding notes or harsh chatter that give their presence away. Long-tailed Tits often form flocks of a dozen or more, and are highly mobile. So learn their characteristic high-pitched squeak, and watch out for their unmistakable silhouette against the branches and twigs above your head. Another tiny bird, the Goldcrest, is also best located by its thin, almost inaudible call.

Winter is a magical time to watch birds, especially if you visit your local woodland on a fine, crisp day.

Listen out for the call of the Nuthatch, which often draws attention to the bird's presence.

If you're really dedicated – and lucky! – you may find a rarity in a tit flock, such as this Pallas's Warbler from Siberia.

Treecreepers often 'tag along' with feeding flocks of other species, especially tits and Goldcrests.

Finally, you can always hope for something a bit more interesting. Coal, Marsh and Willow Tits sometimes join flocks, as do Nuthatch and Treecreeper, though the latter is more likely to be found pursuing a solitary search for food in the crevices of tree-trunks. Lesser Spotted Woodpeckers look far more passerine-like than their larger relatives, and you might even momentarily overlook them, though once seen well they are easy to identify.

Who knows – you may even be lucky enough to find a real rarity amongst the flock – perhaps a Pallas's Warbler or even an American vagrant, like the Black-and-white Warbler that delighted birdwatchers at a Norfolk nature reserve a few winters ago.

LOOKING AND LISTENING: *SPRING*

As the winter gives way to spring, so birds begin to sing, to defend a territory and win a mate. This, in theory at least, should make them easier to find; and in the early spring, when there are fewer leaves on the trees, it does.

But by April and May, as the summer migrants return to our woods and forests, things get a bit more difficult. Not only is there a greater variety of singing birds, but the foliage may now be too thick to see them.

Under these circumstances, there are a number of things you can do to help develop your fieldcraft skills relating to birdsong. First, be patient. You won't be able to see and identify every bird within a few seconds of hearing it, so don't try. Instead, listen carefully to the song and see if you can identify the species on this alone. If you can't, then you'll need to see the bird. But blundering blindly towards the sound is likely to frighten it away. Instead, you need patience and a few useful tips.

Many birds sing from a particular place: sometimes out in the open, such as a roof, treetop or fence post, at other times, deep in dense foliage. Listen carefully, perhaps cupping your hands behind your ears, which helps magnify the sound and pinpoint the direction where it is coming from. Remember, many birds have ventriloquial skills, and often seem to have the ability not only to confuse you regarding direction, but also distance. Most birdsong sounds louder, and therefore closer, than it actually is. The classic example of this is the Corncrake, whose incessant craking song, usually

As the evenings get lighter in late winter, birds like the Blackbird begin singing to mark their territory.

Using your ears can be as important as using your eyes, especially in a woodland habitat.

Birds such as this Reed Warbler are often hard to see as they skulk in their reedbed habitat; so make sure you learn their distinctive song.

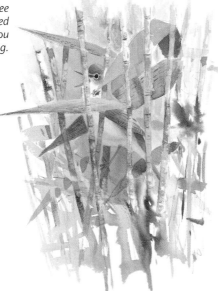

delivered from dense grass, always sounds far closer than the bird itself.

Rapid movement will frighten the bird, so instead try moving slowly a couple of yards to the side of your original position, listening as you go. This should help you work out the rough distance of the bird, and may even enable you to see a bird which was hidden from view. Use your naked eye as well as your binoculars; it often helps you locate tiny movements which should finally reveal the presence of the bird.

The elusive Corncrake is one of the hardest British birds to see: not only do they hide in long grass, they even throw their voice!

This can be frustrating, and you may find that the majority of the time you are unable to locate the mystery songster. But as always, persist: effort and patience really will pay off in the end!

Minsmere RSPB reserve has more habitats concentrated into one small area of land than any other in Britain.

HABITAT

Until Terence Conran used the word to launch his famous furniture store, 'habitat' was largely confined to the vocabulary of professional scientists. Even today, the word has a serious ring to it, and you rarely hear it in birders' day-to-day conversation.

Yet the concept of habitat is central to the way we understand all living creatures, not just birds. The dictionary definition describes it as 'the natural home of an animal or plant', which is fine as far as it goes, but requires a little more explanation to be useful.

Originally, the term 'habitat' referred simply to the specific environment inhabited by a particular organism. However, it soon acquired a broader meaning: the whole environment in which a community of organisms live – for example a mixed woodland, saltmarsh or freshwater lake.

Avocets require a specialised habitat of brackish water in which to feed.

Habitats are formed by the interaction of a complex series of factors, including soil-type, the prevailing climate, altitude, and the presence or absence of water. In turn, these factors influence the plant life, which in turn largely dictates the animal life, including, of course, birds.

Some species of birds require a particular habitat in which to live and raise their young. The Dartford Warbler, for example, is confined as a British

63

breeding bird to dry, lowland heath, though on the Continent it can often be found in less specialised scrubby habitats. The Red-throated Diver, on the other hand, nests exclusively on the edge of small, freshwater lochs in the wilds of Scotland. Other species, like the Woodpigeon, Carrion Crow and Wren, are able to adapt to a wide variety of habitats, and consequently they enjoy a much wider distribution.

Knowing which birds are found in which habitats is an important part of developing your fieldcraft skills. You wouldn't visit a wood to see a Bittern, or a reedbed to see a Yellowhammer, and knowing what to expect enables you immediately to narrow down the possibilities when you come across an unfamiliar bird.

Subtleties of habitats are also vital; for example, you can tell Sedge and Reed Warblers apart on both their plumage features (if you can see them!)

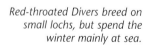
Lochs such as Loch Pityoulish in Scotland are excellent habitat for breeding birds.

and their song. Another key difference is that although they are both found in the same reedbed habitat, Reed Warblers generally perch on the reeds, while Sedge Warblers frequently sing from a perch, such as a small bush or tree. Blackcap and Garden Warbler are both found in the same woodland habitat, but Blackcaps tend to prefer

Red-throated Divers breed on small lochs, but spend the winter mainly at sea.

Heathland like this part of the Suffolk coast has a very specialised birdlife, including Nightjars, Stonechats and a few Dartford Warblers.

denser foliage, while Garden Warblers can be found in more open areas with clearings.

However, being more mobile than many creatures, birds are not always confined to the same habitat the whole year round. Waders which nest on the arctic tundra will spend the winter on coastal estuaries; finches will move out of the woodland edge to spend the winter on farmland; and on migration, birds can turn up in the most unexpected places.

One of the most interesting aspects of a habitat is how quickly it can change, being anything but static. So some habitats, such as heathland, require active management by man to stop them turning into something else. Without human intervention, a heath will soon begin to change into a scrubby woodland, supporting an entirely different (and less specialised) community of plant and animal life.

Habitat is a key concept in the conservation of birds. When it was founded back in the nineteenth century, the RSPB concentrated its efforts on preserving single species like the Great Crested Grebe against persecution. During the twentieth century, however, there was a shift towards conserving wider habitats containing a community of living things. Now, organisations such as the RSPB and The Wildlife Trusts must face up to global issues such as climate change, in order to safeguard habitats for the future.

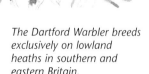

The Dartford Warbler breeds exclusively on lowland heaths in southern and eastern Britain.

65

TIMING

Knowing which birds you will see at a particular time of year is an important part of birding. After all, you wouldn't look for a Cuckoo in winter or Smew in summer – at least not in the British Isles. But another time-related factor can be almost as important – and that's time of day.

If you want to see Wood Warblers, your best chance is to get up early on a fine day in May and visit an oak wood in southern England or Wales.

TIME OF DAY

When I began birding, no one told me that if I wanted to see woodland birds in spring, my best bet would be to get up while it was still dark. So I spent many an unhappy hour wandering aimlessly around apparently suitable habitat, during the middle of the day. Not surprisingly, I didn't see all that many birds.

The first time I really appreciated the joys of dawn birding was on a bright May morning in the New Forest. I couldn't believe my ears: warblers, flycatchers and Redstarts seemed to be competing for my attention, first by song, then as it got lighter, by performing before my eyes. It even made getting up at four a.m. worthwhile!

In a woodland habitat, it's often worth standing in one place and waiting for the birds to come to you.

But even if you can't get out in the field until after sun-up, it's still worth going early. Most songbird activity takes place at the

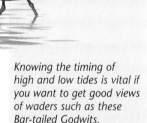

start of the day, and you're far more likely to get good views of a breeding species, or catch a glimpse of a passing migrant, earlier rather than later.

Try to choose your morning carefully: ideally it should be fine and clear, with as little wind as possible, to enable you to see and hear the birds more clearly. Pick your spot, get yourself comfortable (remembering that it can still be very cold, even in May) and wait. You won't be disappointed.

By and large, the middle of the day can be very quiet, especially in woodland habitats, when most birds are resting out of the way of predators. That's the time to head off to more open habitats such as gravel-pits, reservoirs and coastal marshes, where the time of day is less critical.

Evening, too, is a good time to find birds. In spring there is a late reprise of the dawn chorus, while in winter the hour or so before dusk is the time when large flocks of birds head off to their communal roosts. As a child I can still remember seeing long lines of gulls commuting between the local gravel-pits, where they spent the day feeding, and the nearby reservoir, where they roosted each night. Yet it was only seventy-five years ago that a young ornithologist named Max Nicholson followed gulls as they left a Central London park one evening, and discovered where they spent the night!

Knowing the timing of high and low tides is vital if you want to get good views of waders such as these Bar-tailed Godwits.

Time and tide wait for no man, so make sure you check the tide tables before you go!

TIME AND TIDE

Time and tide wait for no man – and no bird either. Many birds, especially waders and other coastal species, govern their behaviour by the tides rather than the actual time of day. At low tide, they take advantage of acres of fertile mud to feed frantically. As the tide begins to rise, they move higher and higher up the shore until they can feed no longer, when they head off, usually to a concentrated high tide roost. They rest here for two or three hours, then as soon as the water begins to drop again, head back to feed. The same pattern is repeated whatever the time of the tides, so waders often feed during the night and sleep during the day, and vice versa.

You can take advantage of this highly predictable behaviour by timing your visit to a particular spot to coincide with the right

Birding at dusk on the Wash at Snettisham in Norfolk: one of the best places in Britain to watch roosting waders.

tides (for which you will need accurate tide tables for that particular locality).

The best time to arrive is generally two or three hours before high tide. Put yourself where the birds will come closer to you as the tide rises; then simply sit and wait. If you've got the timing and position right, you'll get great views; if not, you'll get wet feet and see nothing!

Alternatively, you can visit a high tide roost and simply wait for the birds to leave the surrounding mudflats and fly in. At places like Snettisham in Norfolk and Elmley in Kent you may see literally thousands of waders, all concentrated together in a huge flock to avoid predators. Another tip: make sure you pick a 'spring' tide, which tends to occur with a new or full moon. These tides maximise the rise in water levels and give you the best chance of seeing large numbers of birds.

Smew are exclusively a winter visitor to Britain, usually arriving in December and leaving in March.

TIME OF YEAR

One small word of warning: you can pick the highest tide of the lot, and the best position, and you still won't see anything – if you're there at the wrong time of year. Time of year is absolutely crucial for the birder, and it's not simply a question of knowing that winter is good for ducks and geese, or that spring sees the arrival of Swallows and Swifts.

Brent Geese can be found most of the year, though most head north to breed in the Arctic during the summer months.

There are many subtle differences between the seasons, and these also depend on your location and the kind of birds you're looking for. Also, timing may not always be what you might expect. By and large, birds' seasons start and finish earlier than ours, so courtship displays associated with spring may begin as early as January, while birdsong may be over in some places by June – even though it's still 'spring'. Autumn (or to be more accurate, 'return') migration can begin as early as late June, when non-breeding waders head back south from the Arctic, while winter visitors may begin arriving in early October, long before the first frosts.

The Cuckoo is exclusively a summer visitor, arriving in late April and heading off in July.

On the other hand, birds can be late to leave as well. Wintering Brent Geese often hang around well into May, even early June, while I've seen House Martins as late as the third week of November!

'Summer visitors' vary dramatically in their arrival dates, with the first Sand Martins and Blackcaps reaching our shores in March, while Spotted Flycatchers may not get here until June! Once Cuckoos

Small birds such as Wrens often respond to pishing and squeaking noises made by humans.

have deposited their eggs they are off back to Africa – sometimes only a month or two after they have arrived; while some species such as the Chiffchaff, once exclusively a summer migrant, now spend the whole year here. So it's important to learn the differences between species, so that next time you see a small green warbler in March you know it's a Chiffchaff rather than a Willow Warbler – even if it isn't singing!

PISHING

It sounds like a nasty medical condition, but in fact pishing is a time-honoured technique for getting a good sighting of an elusive bird, especially in autumn and winter. Like many trends, it started in the USA, where for many years birdwatchers (or birders, as they prefer to be called) have used it to attract small birds.

It works like this. You purse your lips and place them against the back of your hand. Then, you begin to make 'kissing' noises. With luck, the bird's curiosity is aroused, and it emerges from the bush in front of you and performs in front of your eyes.

But why? One theory is that pishing sounds like the contact calls made by small birds to attract other members of their flock to food, or perhaps warning of danger, so they come to see what all the fuss is about. Either that, or as Bill Oddie suggests in his *Little Black Bird Book*, they just want to have a good laugh at you making a fool of yourself.

In fact, pishing does seem to work, especially with tits and American wood-warblers. This explains why you see otherwise sensible people standing by bushes in the Isles of Scilly, kissing the back of their hand.

Pishing may look silly – but it really works!

If you are too embarrassed to try the traditional method of pishing, you may prefer to adopt the more refined, British approach. You don't have to kiss your hand – just make a repeated 'pish-pish-pish' noise. It doesn't work, of course, but at least it saves you trying to explain what you were doing to a passing police officer.

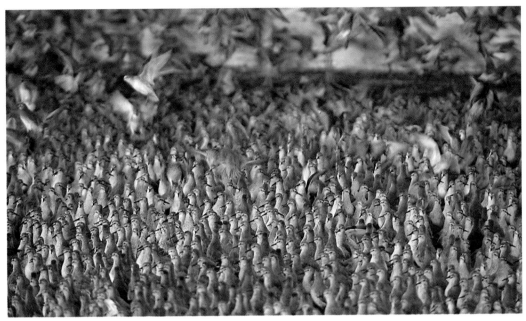

Counting waders such as this Knot flock takes plenty of practice!

COUNTING BIRDS

How do you count birds? Add up the legs and divide by two!

In fact, counting birds is harder than you might think, for several reasons. First, birds are more mobile than say trees or buildings. Second, they don't just move around, but frequently hide – either deliberately or accidentally. And finally, many species gather together in flocks numbering in the hundreds, thousands or even tens of thousands.

Counting birds is a combination of science and art, with a little bit of magic thrown in. The science comes from understanding how birds of a particular species behave, and making allowances for this. For example, in the breeding season, male songbirds like the Dunnock or Great Tit hold territories, and defend these against intruders by singing from a prominent place. So marking down the positions of the singing birds, especially on more than one visit, is likely to give a reasonable estimation of the number of pairs present.

The art comes from learning the habits of birds, enabling you to seek out those that favour a particular feeding spot, or only emerge at dawn or dusk, for example. Counting birds like the Water Rail takes reserves of patience that might tax a saint, and

Songbirds such as the Dunnock are best counted by mapping their territories by listening for their song in spring.

Birds which habitually spend time in flocks, such as these Rooks, are fairly easy to count.

even the most knowledgeable and persistent observer will only be able to make a rough estimate of the number of birds present at any one time.

Don't lose heart – most birds are a lot easier to count than these elusive skulkers! But how do you go about counting a huge flock of waders or wildfowl, or a large group of gulls or Woodpigeons passing overhead, before they pass out of sight?

The first thing to do is take a split-second to make a rough estimate, remembering that you are likely to underestimate by as much as 50%. Then count the first ten birds – or if the flock is particularly large, the first 100 – and use this as your baseline for 'guestimating' the rest. If you have the time, start again from the other end, once again counting in 'blocks' of ten or a hundred. With a little practice, you should soon get the knack.

DETECTIVE WORK

One of the most pleasurable aspects of watching birds is the chance it gives you to indulge in some good old-fashioned detective work. Wherever you are, whatever the time of year, the ability to think logically and solve problems always applies.

Take a regular walk around your local patch in early autumn. You know the resident birds: which species, and perhaps even how many individuals are present. You know which bird calls you expect to hear. So as you walk round, you are looking and listening out for something different. At first, it's easy to walk right past, before you realise that what you've just heard is an unfamiliar call, or at least, unfamiliar in that place, at that time of year.

The next step is, as always, to track the bird down and put an identity to it. Your detective work may be rewarded with the sight of something unusual, such as a passing migrant or even something rarer; or you may be disappointed to find that after all it's just one of the familiar species, giving an unusual call.

On less familiar territory, playing detective is even more important. As you walk through any new habitat you should constantly be asking yourself 'What do I expect to see in a place like this, at this time of year, at this particular time of day, and in these weather conditions?' You'll be amazed at how often your initial hunch is proved correct, and as if by magic, the predicted birds appear.

top tip

GET A LOCAL PATCH

The very best way to gain experience of a wide range of species is to find a local patch – a place you visit on a regular basis to get to know the birds that live there. Keep detailed records of different species and how many individuals are present. You'll soon gain a real insight into the behaviour and habits of your local birds.

These birders on the Scilly Isles will have to use all their detective skills to identify some of the American rarities that can appear in autumn.

But like any detective work, you can be proved utterly wrong. There's always something you didn't expect, didn't predict, shouldn't really be there anyway. One warm day in April I remember seeing a small bird with a white rump in the middle of the road by my local patch – it looked like a Wheatear, because that's just what it was! Another time, on a freezing day in winter, I heard a familiar call, and realised a few seconds later that it was my first record of a Redshank there. That's one of the great pleasures of being a birdwatcher – you never quite know what will turn up next.

Detective work can also pay off for the birds: a few years ago birders noticed a major decline in Whitethroat numbers, which turned out to be because of droughts in Africa. Fortunately the species has since recovered in numbers.

BIRDS' NESTS AND EGGS

Finding a bird's nest is always an exciting experience, however common the species. But our urge to share the joys of avian reproduction should always be tempered with a little caution.

The most obvious thing to avoid is causing a bird to desert the nest altogether. This is unlikely with most species in parks and gardens, or other places where they are familiar with people. However, individual birds may be more nervous than others, so it's best to play it safe. If you come across a nest unexpectedly, and the sitting bird moves off, get away from the site as quickly and quietly as possible, to allow it to return.

If a bird stays off the eggs for some time, it is possible that they may go so cold they fail to hatch. If there are chicks, then they may not withstand exposure to the elements, especially if the weather is particularly cold or wet.

Flushing a bird from the nest is also an open invitation to predators to come and enjoy a tasty meal, especially opportunistic feeders like the Jay or Magpie. Even if the bird

Grey Herons are very early nesters: look out for breeding activity from the New Year onwards!

The pale blue eggs of the Song Thrush appear to provide little or no camouflage against predators.

This Magpie has discovered a nest and is making a quick meal of the eggs.

returns rapidly, you may have drawn unnecessary attention to its presence. Some species are more prone to desertion than others. Red-throated Divers nest on the edges of small lochs, and are so well camouflaged that it is easy not to notice them until it is too late. Along with more than 80 other species, Black-throated Divers are protected by Schedule I of the 1981 Wildlife and Countryside Act, which means that disturbing them unnecessarily is against the law. This applies to birdwatchers just as much as anyone else, so beware!

As rare breeders Black-throated Divers are protected under Schedule 1 of the Wildlife and Countryside Act, and may not be disturbed at or near the nest.

A Marsh Tit brings food to its nest. The nest is usually located in natural cavities such as this hole in a tree. They also occupy rotten stumps and holes in walls.

Two other activities that can cause a bird to desert are tape-luring and photography. The effect of tape-luring (using a recording of a bird in order to flush it out of cover) is controversial, with some people claiming that it rarely does any harm, while others believe it should be banned. The truth probably lies somewhere between the two, but if in doubt, don't do it!

Nest photography, when carried out sensitively by professionals, is unlikely to cause harm. Remember, you need a permit to photograph any Schedule I species at or even near the nest.

Finally, remember that the small but ruthless band of egg-collectors will use any information about rare breeding birds they can get hold of. So if you do come across a rare or out-of-range species, even if you only suspect that it might be nesting, keep quiet about it until you've consulted your local county bird recorder.

The fear of being branded an egg-collector means that many of today's birdwatchers have rarely enjoyed a really close look at a bird's nest and eggs. But with due care and attention it is perfectly possible to do so without harming the bird's chances of breeding success. Make sure that you do not damage any vegetation around the nest, making it more accessible to predators. Don't spend too long looking at a nest. And avoid disturbance during cold or wet weather, which may lead to eggs failing to hatch, or the chicks dying of exposure.

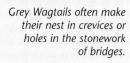

Grey Wagtails often make their nest in crevices or holes in the stonework of bridges.

When you do take a close-up look at a clutch of eggs, you can only admire the beauty and subtlety of their coloration and patterning. They may be spotted, like those of the Song Thrush; blotched, like the Magpie; or streaked, like the House Sparrow.

In some cases, this patterning has given rise to folk-names: in many country areas the Yellowhammer was known as the 'Writing Lark' or 'Scribbling Lark', due to the dark, pencil-like markings on its eggs. These markings are derived from pigment secreted in the female's oviduct (the passage through which the egg passes during the laying process), and only appear just before laying. The purpose of such markings is to provide camouflage against predators, although it is hard to believe that an observant Jay or Magpie wouldn't spot the sky-blue background of a Song Thrush's egg.

The Long-tailed Tit makes a beautiful, intricate nest out of moss, spiders' webs and feathers.

Not all birds' eggs are subtly camouflaged. Many species which nest in holes, like the Sand Martin and Kingfisher, have white eggs – presumably because predators visiting these nests hunt by touch, not sight, so camouflage would confer no evolutionary advantage.

Honing your nest-finding skills may be unfashionable nowadays, but it does add another dimension to your birding, and is part and parcel of fieldcraft. As long as you are careful, and follow a sensible code of conduct, the birds will not come to harm, and you will enjoy a quite unique experience.

Once the eggs have hatched, this parent Wren has its work cut out feeding a brood of hungry chicks.

top tip

LOOK OUT FOR NESTS

The breeding season begins as early as January for some species, so keep your eyes peeled for signs of nest-building.

4 NEXT STEPS

Once you have been birding for a while, you will want to broaden your interest and develop your hobby. You don't have to go far to do this: attracting birds to your garden will provide you with endless opportunities to get to know some familiar species in greater depth, by observing their behaviour. The next logical step is to get a 'local patch': somewhere you can visit regularly and get to know the birds that live there. Finally, you can venture farther afield, visiting nature reserves and other birding sites on your own, with friends, or with a bird club. As you develop your birding skills you may want to get yourself a telescope, visit a birdwatching fair, photograph birds, go seawatching or even become a twitcher! Ultimately, you can spread your wings even further by going on your first birding trip abroad.

GARDEN BIRDING

Britain's gardens are a vital refuge for our birds. As natural habitats such as hedgerows, meadows and woodlands continue to disappear, your garden can be a vital oasis, helping birds to survive and maintain their numbers. But we don't just help garden birds for their sake. Watching birds in your garden provides endless hours of pleasure and delight, and helps you learn more about them too.

It's a great way to learn the techniques of identification and fieldcraft, and to learn more about bird behaviour, which you can observe at really close quarters. So don't be too eager to venture to wild, exotic places in search of birds – there may be more than enough in your own backyard!

So much for why you should attract birds to your garden – how do you do so? However large or small your garden, and whether it's in a city centre, a quiet suburb or the heart of the countryside, the same fundamental rules apply. Birds may vary from place to place and garden to garden, but their needs do not!

Birds are attracted to a garden by four main things:

- Food: to provide the energy needed to survive, especially during harsh winter weather or summer drought.
- Water: to drink and to bathe.
- Shelter: places to roost at night, and to build a nest and raise young during the breeding season.
- Safety: an environment where they can carry out these activities without danger from poisoning, pests or predators.

There are several stages in the process of creating a 'bird-friendly' garden:

- Planning: you need to decide what you are going to do, how, and by when.
- Planting: to create areas where birds can roost and nest, and plants which produce fruit or berries, or attract insects for the birds to eat.
- Feeding: to provide a range of food to attract a wide variety of different species, with different feeding requirements, throughout the year.
- Providing: nest-sites such as nestboxes, for birds to use as a substitute when natural sites are not available or are in short supply.

Bird baths provide an essential place to drink and bathe for birds such as this Starling.

There are several excellent books on how to attract birds to your garden (*see* Further Reading).

By the way, another way to make the most of your garden birds is to keep a diary of what you see in, around and over your garden. I moved house recently, and have been making entries in a small hardback notebook of the birds I see. It's an excellent discipline, and as with all your field notebooks, it will give you great pleasure as you re-read it in years to come.

LOCAL PATCH WORK

The term 'local patch' first crept into birding conversations sometime during the 1980s. As the name suggests, it refers to a fairly small, self-contained area which you visit regularly, in order to build up a picture of the resident and visiting birdlife.

A local patch can be more or less anywhere, from a windswept offshore island to an inner-city park – so long as it contains at least one habitat attractive to birds. Almost as important is easy access, so you can make frequent and regular visits. There's not much point having an excellent patch half-an-hour's drive away, which you can only visit every other weekend.

So how do you choose your local patch? That very much depends on where you live. You may be spoilt for choice, in which case the main factor may be the presence of other birdwatchers. It's always nice to be a pioneer, so why not seek out somewhere new? But if, like me, you live in the suburbs of a big city, choice may be more limited.

My advice would be to explore the area within a mile or so of your home, on foot or by bicycle. Look for a self-contained, 'island' habitat which attracts passing birds, such as a disused gravel-pit, small woodland or park.

Cormorants are becoming much more common inland, so you may see them on your local patch.

Make a couple of reconnaissance visits at different times of the day, and note down what you see there, not just which species, but numbers of birds too. See how long it takes you to cover the area thoroughly: between 30 minutes and an hour is probably the optimum, especially if you're planning to visit the patch on your way to or from work, or at weekends.

When it comes to patch work, dedication is important – it's not much use only going once or twice a month. Regular visits, say two or three times a week over a period of time, can yield far more than you might

Try to visit your local patch at least once a week – more often if you have the time.

imagine. I spent three years watching a small disused reservoir by the River Thames in south-west London, and saw almost 90 species there, including Yellow-legged and Mediterranean Gulls, Tawny Owl, and seven different species of warbler.

Dedicated patch work over the years can eventually produce some real rarities, as the editor of *Birdwatch* magazine, Dominic Mitchell, discovered when he found a singing male Subalpine Warbler on his local patch in east London!

But rare visitors aren't the real reason for regular patch work. The most satisfying part is the sense that these are 'your' birds, with every arrival, departure or newly-hatched young being witnessed and recorded by you personally. Even common birds take on a special significance: for me, a flock of 75 Cormorants, a spring fall of Chiffchaffs, and fabulous views of a family of Little Grebes gave me special pleasure.

Taken together, the thousands of regular patch-workers also provide a major weapon in the battle to conserve valuable habitats. My old local patch would have disappeared years ago, if it hadn't been for a dedicated group of people who campaigned to turn it into a local nature reserve.

One of the pleasures of 'patch work' is that you get to see birds you might normally overlook, like this Little Grebe with a chick.

In a world where every piece of decent habitat seems to be under threat, patch work can help to preserve somewhere special for future generations of birdwatchers to enjoy. And in the meantime, there's always something new to see.

TAKING YOUR BIRDING FURTHER

This juvenile Green Sandpiper is the kind of species you will begin to encounter when you explore farther afield.

After you've been watching birds on your local patch for a while, you're bound to get the urge to explore farther afield, to broaden your birding experience.

But where do you start? Well, it's a good idea to build on the knowledge of birds you've already gained on your patch. If you regularly watch a freshwater habitat such as a small lake or gravel pit, pay a visit to a larger reservoir in the area. There, you'll find a greater number of birds you already know, as well as less familiar species. You'll also have to get used to watching birds at greater distances than before, so you may need to buy or borrow a telescope.

If your local patch is a wooded habitat, try exploring a more extensive mixed woodland, such as one of the royal forests. Once again, you're likely to see a greater variety of species than on your home territory: perhaps four or five kinds of tit instead of two or three, or a scarcer

Coastal sites such as Rye Harbour Nature Reserve usually hold a good range of species.

species such as Lesser Spotted Woodpecker or Hawfinch.

After a while, you'll be itching to explore even farther afield, perhaps paying a visit to a coastal estuary or saltmarsh in search of wintering waders and wildfowl. Remember that not only will some of the species you see be unfamiliar, but that you'll also be observing new kinds of behaviour. So always take a field notebook, and record interesting sightings as well as listing the different species you see.

Take time to get to know each new habitat. Visit at different times of the day, and at different seasons, to experience the full variety of birds found there. And remember, a thorough knowledge of bird habitats, gained over a period of time, will pay dividends in the future.

To see a Lesser Spotted Woodpecker you will need to visit a mature woodland.

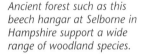

Ancient forest such as this beech hangar at Selborne in Hampshire support a wide range of woodland species.

'Where to watch' guides are almost as essential as your field guide, helping to find the very best places to watch birds.

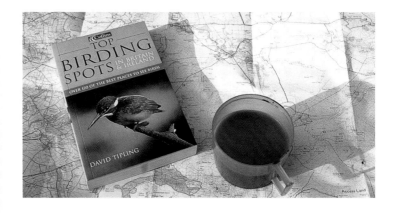

'WHERE TO WATCH' GUIDES

Back in the 1960s, if you wanted to know the best places to watch birds, you had to rely on local knowledge. Apart from famous national hotspots such as the Scillies and Cley, and the network of RSPB reserves like Loch Garten and Minsmere, many good bird sites were a closely-guarded secret, accessible only to those with inside knowledge.

Then, almost overnight, things changed. In 1967, John Gooders published a modest little volume simple entitled *Where to Watch Birds*. Like all brilliant ideas, it was dead simple. He listed more than 500 sites, up and down the country, and the birds found there at different times of the year. To help you find the sites yourself, he added directions or a map. The 'where to watch' guide was born.

Since then, Gooders' own guide has gone into many editions and sold thousands of copies. Later on, he developed the idea into 'Where to Watch Birds in Britain and Europe', the latest edition of which includes North Africa, the Middle East, and even the Gambia!

Site guides are very helpful if you want to track down rare breeding species such as the Bittern.

Other publishers soon jumped onto the bandwagon, with Nigel Redman and Simon Harrap's *Birdwatching in Britain: a site-by-site guide* (soon to be republished) and A & C Black's excellent series of region-by-region guides to the British Isles. The latter have the advantage of covering a much smaller area, such as Devon and Cornwall, or East Anglia, and can therefore feature many more sites in considerable detail. Recently, publishers have gone still farther afield, with guides to various regions of Europe, and even South America, Asia and Africa!

'Where to watch' guides have, on balance, been a good

thing for birdwatchers. After all, anything that enables people to develop their skills and extend their horizons must be beneficial, and few would want a return to the bad old days. However, the downside of these guides is that they can encourage a 'follow-the-crowd' mentality, with birdwatchers concentrating at 'honeypot' sites to the exclusion of other, equally good ones. The move towards local patch work over the last few years may be a reaction against this herd-like mentality.

So if you're new to birding, by all means buy these guides, but before you use them, heed a few words of warning. Long lists of birds to be seen at a particular site often include everything that has ever occurred there! So don't take everything you read as gospel truth, or you're likely to be disappointed. Also, some shy species, like the Bittern, may be listed as present at a site, but that doesn't mean you're going to see one on your very first visit – or even your fifth!

Make sure you're visiting the site at the right time of day, however spectacular the dawn chorus in a mixed woodland, if you don't get there until after lunch you're not likely to see very much. Finally, don't allow the list of birds to blinker you to other possibilities: the writers of these guides aren't all-knowing, and you may be lucky enough to stumble upon something unexpected that isn't included in your guide.

Bempton Cliffs RSPB reserve in Yorkshire is a well-known hotspot for birds and birders.

Getting guidance from a more experienced birder is a great way to learn.

GETTING A MENTOR

In the world of business, there's a buzzword doing the rounds. Employees, whether they're chairman of the board or the office junior, are advised to get themselves a 'mentor'. Named after a trusted adviser in Homer's Odyssey, a mentor is there to guide you, enabling you to do your job better, and enjoy it more. It's not a bad idea for birders, either. If you're just starting out, why not get yourself a mentor? Knowing a more experienced observer who can help you identify difficult birds, guide you round unfamiliar habitats, and answer questions, can be a godsend.

So how do you find this latter-day combination of saint and oracle? With a bit of luck, you may already know someone who's been birding longer than you have, and can give you the benefit of his or her expertise. Or perhaps you regularly come across other birdwatchers on your local patch. Next time you get into conversation, ask them questions: not just 'what's about?' but why birds behave the way they do, or how to identify a problem species. They may not be able to answer all your queries, but they'll be flattered to be asked. If you seem to be the only birder in your area, seek out your local bird club – there are bound to be some like-minded souls there.

A word of warning, though. Don't treat your mentor as an all-knowing expert simply there to tell you the facts. Get them to challenge your knowledge, and test you on your growing skills in identification and fieldcraft. Hopefully it won't be long before you'll be able to teach them a thing or two in return!

BIRD CLUBS

Not everyone has access to a car, and getting to many birding hotspots by public transport can be a logistical nightmare. One way round this problem is to join your local bird club. They will almost certainly run a series of reasonably priced day-trips to the

Joining a bird club is a good way to meet other birders: this is an outing to the Farne Islands in summer.

very places you want to visit. Some will be by coach, others in shared cars. All you need to do is get in touch with the meetings secretary, or whoever is running that particular trip, and let them know you need a lift.

Of course, there are drawbacks. You may find yourself stuck with the world's most boring couple, who drive at twenty-nine miles an hour and get to the site long after everyone else has moved on. And even when you get there, your enjoyment may be spoilt by the endless 'traveller's tales', as the more seasoned club members go on and on about their latest trip to Turkey or Morocco.

But consider the advantages of bird clubs. It's a lot cheaper than public transport: even a long-distance coach trip is unlikely to cost more than a few pounds, and more local trips are usually free. Not all club members are boring: you can learn a lot from a more experienced birder if you're willing to listen. And being in a small group often maximises your chances of seeing the birds.

So how do you get in touch with your local bird club? If you've got a recent copy of your county bird report, it will include a contact address. You could also try asking at your local library. Finally, the annual *Birdwatcher's Yearbook and Diary* includes a list of bird clubs up and down the country, as well as stacks of other useful information (*see* Further Reading).

TELESCOPES

When you begin birding, especially if you spend most of your time watching birds in your garden or on your local patch, a pair of binoculars is all you need to see and identify them. But as you begin to explore farther afield, you may soon become frustrated. If you only use binoculars, birds don't always come close enough for you to see their plumage details and sometimes they're so far away you can't even begin to identify them.

When that happens, it's time to think about buying a telescope. Scopes don't just allow closer views of distant birds. They also give you a rock-steady view of plumage detail, without the inevitable movement you get when looking through binoculars. And when you view a bird in close-up, you can appreciate its aesthetic qualities much better through the lens of a scope.

The annual British Birdwatching Fair, held at The Wildlife Trusts's Egleton Nature Reserve at Rutland Water, is a great place to test out telescopes before you part with your money.

When choosing a telescope, the most important things to consider are power, weight and price, all of which need to be taken into account before you part with your money.

- *Power* Unlike binoculars, telescopes come in two parts: the body (with the large objective lens at the front), and the eyepiece, which can be either a fixed lens or a zoom. Zoom eyepieces allow you to increase power from 20x to 40x, or even 60x, without changing the eyepiece – very convenient if you want to get a closer view – but with an inevitable loss of quality and narrower field of view. Fixed eyepieces are almost always better quality, with a sharper image and wider field of view than a zoom. However, being unable to 'zoom in' on a distant bird can sometimes be frustrating. Personally, I use two eyepieces: a 20x wide angle for normal use, with a 50x wide angle in reserve for those times when I need more power.

- *Weight* Some of the best scopes are quite heavy and bulky, so you may prefer to choose a smaller, lightweight model, even if this means a slight compromise on quality. Remember that you won't just be carrying the scope itself, but the tripod, too. Try out a few different tripods, making sure the legs are easy to put up and down, and that the pan and tilt movement is smooth. Ideally choose a model with a fluid head for ease of movement.

- *Price* This is perhaps the main factor governing your choice of telescope. The cheapest decent scope plus tripod combination will set you back at least £200–£300 and you can pay well over £1000 for a top model. My advice is to buy the best body you can afford, with a single, fixed, wide-angle eyepiece (either 20x or 30x). You can always buy extra eyepieces later on.

A telescope should help you get close up views of species such as the Sparrowhawk (above) and Kingfisher (below).

Another factor, especially at the top end of the market, is whether to go for a 'straight' or 'angled' eyepiece. For many years a straight eyepiece, which juts out from the body in the conventional manner, was the only style available. Then manufacturers began to bring out models with the option of an angled eyepiece, jutting out at a 45° angle to the body. The angled eyepiece takes a while to get used to, but has two major advantages. First, it enables you to watch high-flying birds such as soaring raptors without contorting your body in order to do so. Second, if you regularly go birding with a companion or partner who is shorter or taller than you, there is no need to keep adjusting the height of the tripod when taking turns to look through the scope.

A scope is also essential for seawatching.

Shy birds like these Smew usually keep their distance; so using a telescope to view them may be essential.

Before you buy, it's vital to try out a range of scopes in the field. Many of the retailers who advertise in the monthly birding magazines hold regular outdoor events, enabling you to try out a range of scopes and eyepieces under realistic conditions. In particular, check the sharpness of image (at the centre and the edges), the field of view, and how quickly and easily you can focus. If it is possible, carry out the test in poor light conditions, when differences in quality are most apparent.

Like binoculars, once you get out in the field, using a telescope needs practice. One of the hardest things to get used to is looking through just one eye. Try not to fully close the other, as you may find it 'mists up', making it hard to switch back to binoculars. Practise quick focusing, and locating birds in different habitats and situations. Soon, looking through a scope will seem as natural as using your binoculars.

CENSUS WORK

No, not the people who come to your door every ten years and ask personal questions. In birding terms, censuses are something *you* do. They're a way of putting something back into your hobby, by finding out more about bird populations, and so help to conserve and protect them.

In Britain, most bird censuses are run by the British Trust for Ornithology (BTO). The best-known are the regular Atlas surveys of our breeding and wintering birds, which are vital in helping to monitor changes in our birdlife.

Other early-warning systems are provided by more detailed census work, such as the Common Birds Census, a survey of regular breeding birds in a variety of habitats which has now been running for over 30 years.

You don't have to have stacks of spare time, or travel to distant places, to take part in a BTO census. The new Garden BirdWatch Survey, as its name suggests, monitors visitors to gardens, and has yielded some fascinating results. These include a notable increase in the numbers of wintering Blackcaps, and the emergence of Siskins as a regular garden visitor. The survey also reveals decreases amongst some common birds, notably the Song Thrush, which a couple of years ago dropped out of the top ten garden birds for the very first time.

Census work has enabled birders to discover changes in the population of our common birds: Siskins (top) have increased, Blackbirds (middle) have a stable population, while Song Thrushes (left) are declining in numbers.

BIRDFAIRS

'Birdfairs', or to give them their proper name, 'Birdwatching Fairs', are a relatively recent phenomenon. The original, and still the best birdfair began when two men, Tim Appleton and Martin Davies, met for a drink in a pub in the heart of England. As a result, they set up the first British Birdwatching Fair, an event which, like Topsy, has grown and grown.

The annual fair, which takes place for three days every August at The Wildlife Trusts's Egleton Nature Reserve by Rutland Water in the East Midlands, is the highlight of the birding year for many people. It's a combination of trade fair, social event and festival – like the Chelsea Flower Show and Glastonbury combined, only with birds. In fact, although the nearby reserve is excellent for birding (and plays host to some of England's first breeding Ospreys) the fair is so eventful that very few people ever manage to spend time watching birds! The alternative attractions include lectures, quizzes, light-hearted panel games and music (usually supplied by the country whose conservation projects are being supported that year). Also the chance to try and buy a huge range of optics, books (new and second-hand), clothing, bird food and feeders; book a birding trip of a lifetime; or simply sit in the sun and enjoy a beer and a chat with fellow enthusiasts.

Ospreys are one of the main attractions at Rutland Water, site of the annual British Birdwatching Fair.

The original and still the best: the annual British Birdwatching Fair is held at Rutland Water every August.

When the Birdfair began, most of the exhibitors were local, or at least British. Now it is a truly global event, with representatives from every continent and almost every well-known birding site in the world. The effects of the Birdfair are global; with more than one million pounds having been donated to specific conservation projects over the years, from Vietnam to Cuba and Poland to Brazil. Now, there are smaller birdfairs in various parts of Britain, as well as abroad: all the offspring of the 'big daddy' of them all.

For the first twenty years or so that I was birding, there was nowhere you could go to meet other like-minded souls, in fact the hobby had a bit of a reputation for being cliquey and insular. Now, all that has changed.

So if you haven't been, I highly recommend it. The dates are usually the third weekend of August (from Friday to Sunday), but for details *see* Further Reading.

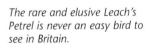

top tip

TRAVEL FARTHER AFIELD

You've got your binoculars, notebook and field guide; you've found yourself a local patch; your letterbox is stuffed with bird magazines and newsletters and the birds are flocking to your garden to feed. So what next? It's time to spread your wings, and explore farther afield: either at home or abroad. Try going on a birding tour: whether you choose a week in Mallorca or a month in Antarctica, it's sure to be an unforgettable experience.

LISTING

Most birders keep lists. The basic one is your 'life list' – all the species you have ever seen (at first, only in Britain, later, as you travel more and more, for the whole world!). In addition, many birders keep a 'year list', of birds they see in this country during a calendar year. Some people frown on listing, seeing it as a trivial pastime that reduces birding to the level of train-spotting. But a year list does have its uses: if only to spur you to visit a variety of habitats and locations in all four seasons, to try to fill in the gaps. Year listing can also add interest to an otherwise dull day's birding, and always brings a frisson of excitement to days out during the early part of the year, when each new location is likely to put a few species onto the list.

The rare and elusive Leach's Petrel is never an easy bird to see in Britain.

I always start off quite well, spending New Year's Day around the West London gravel-pits, usually nursing a hangover. A visit to the North Kent marshes, and a February weekend in Norfolk, bring the list over the 120 mark without too much trouble. Then spring brings another clutch of 'ticks' as the returning migrants arrive. One year I even made it to the magic

If you want a big 'year-list' you'll need to visit a seabird colony in summer.

American vagrants such as this Northern Parula are a dream find for any birder, and will attract crowds of twitchers eager to get the bird onto their life list.

200 mark by the middle of May, thanks to a memorable trip to Scotland. But by July I always seem to lose interest, and despite a late flurry in October, I generally end the year on a fairly pitiful total. Every New Year's Day I resolve to do it properly – maybe one year I shall.

There is a lot of nonsense talked about listing. Some birdwatchers seem to suggest that making any kind of list relegates you to the status of an uncaring philistine, as if listing were incompatible with every other aspect of watching birds.

To set the record straight, keeping a record of the birds you see, and making a special effort to encounter new species, will not prevent you being involved in surveys, conservation work, or taking an interest in bird habits and behaviour. Neither will it make you blind. So go ahead – and don't feel guilty!

There is always a special magic about seeing a bird for the first time: however common-or-garden the species, however ordinary the setting. I still remember the thrill of seeing my first Great Crested Grebe on the disused gravel-pit near my home, back in the late 1960s. It was there, a year or so later, I saw my first Goldeneye – a splendid male – bringing my life-list up to somewhere around the fifty-mark, at a guess.

Today, at a guess, my British list must be around the 370-mark, and, because I rarely go twitching nowadays, is unlikely to get much longer. I have recently started keeping a world list, but as I've only seen about 1,500 of the 10,000 or so species found on the globe, it's not going to break any records.

The nice thing about my British list is that I can truly say I can remember virtually every species (apart from the few dozen I saw before I was old enough to remember!) Looking back over your life-list never fails to bring back memories: everything from the mythical rarity to getting to grips with that bogey bird (in my case, a Bittern at Leighton Moss).

Bewick's Swan (above) and Whooper Swan (below) are two species of wildfowl likely to be seen at sites such as Slimbridge.

Then there are the gaps. The wonderful thing about a list is that these gaps represent the promise of days to come, when you finally come across a bird you've always wanted to see. My 'bogey bird' is Leach's Petrel, which despite much effort I've never yet managed to catch up with. So if your list is full of blank spaces, look on the bright side: you'll get a huge amount of pleasure filling them in!

Many birders start the year with a visit to a wetland site such as the WWT centre at Slimbridge, where they will be able to add a good range of species to their 'year list'.

Seeing a Long-tailed Skua is a memorable event for any birder – twitcher or not!

TWITCHING

Twitching is defined as going purposely to see a rare bird that someone else has discovered: be it 500 miles away or in the garden next door. A few people consider twitchers to be the birding equivalent of lager-louts; social pariahs whose very existence besmirches the good name of a once respectable pastime. Fortunately most twitchers are thick-skinned enough to cope with such bigoted nonsense, and like all birders, they enjoy their hobby – which after all is the purpose of doing it in the first place.

Of course, every one of us is a twitcher to some extent. When you go to see the Avocets at Minsmere, or the Ospreys at Loch Garten, you're twitching. But some highly respected birders do make it a point of principle not to go to see 'other people's rarities', but to find their own rare birds. It's a laudable aim, but you have to be pretty self-disciplined to turn your back on a rare bird just spotted by the bloke sitting next to you in a hide!

Some criticisms of twitching are justified. The use of precious fossil fuels to travel thousands of miles to see one storm-blown vagrant does seem a little irresponsible; while in the past twitchers have trampled crops and insulted local birders (and worse still, non-birders). However, bad behaviour was always the province of a tiny minority, and in recent years twitchers seem to have behaved very well. One of the spin-offs of hundreds of people coming to see a rare bird is that money is often raised for a local conservation project.

But ultimately, twitching is a sport, and like many sports, one of the main reasons for participating is the social side. Lifelong

A big twitch can attract hundreds, even thousands of people, all eager to see the rare bird.

friendships have been made while twitching – hardly surprising as spending several days in the backseat of a car with your fellow birder will either make you firm friends or lifelong enemies. And in a world where we should respect other people's passions, twitching is, as the late Douglas Adams might have said, mostly harmless.

Although common in mainland Europe, the Serin is still a rare visitor to Britain, and any sighting will attract crowds of twitchers.

PHONELINES AND PAGERS

So if you do want to go twitching, what will you need? Well, apart from the usual birding paraphernalia, there are two high-tech products you should know about. The first are the premium rate bird information lines. These began in the late 1980s, as a response to the growing demand for up-to-the-minute information on the whereabouts of rare birds. The original was Birdline, set up by a group of birdwatchers. It is still going strong, and still sets the high standards of speed and reliability essential for any rare bird information line.

Nowadays there are also regional phonelines covering the whole of the British Isles, which carry details of relatively common birds, arrivals of migrants, and even information on dragonflies and cetaceans (whales and dolphins)!

Like twitching, phonelines do have their critics. The main objection is that they take the fun out of birding: if you know what you're going to see before you get to a particular site, you might as well visit a zoo, as the argument runs. On the other hand, you don't have to phone them, or you can even do as one well-known birder and television personality does: use the information they give out to avoid sites where birders will congregate!

Once a common British breeding bird, the Red-backed Shrike is now only seen during spring and autumn passage.

Phonelines are great, but you may need to ring them several times a day, which over time can prove expensive. A few years ago the idea of using pagers to send up-to-the-minute information about rare birds was thought of by a group of Norfolk birders. Today, your pager service can even be personalised, so that if a 'mega-gripper' (i.e. ultra rarity) turns up, the alarm will override any instructions and still go off – at any time of day or night, and wherever you are!

Pagers can be annoying to other birders, especially if the owner sets them to go off audibly instead of vibrating discreetly in his or her pocket. There's nothing worse than sitting in a hide on a dull day with few birds about, only for some idiot to yell 'Oh my God! Pacific Swift at Cley!' I know – I've been there…

For details of phonelines see Useful Addresses.

BIRD RINGING AND OBSERVATORIES

Ringing birds has a long pedigree. It is believed that the Ancient Greeks tied coloured threads to the legs of migrating Swallows in the hope that they might discover where they spent the winter, and medieval falconers marked their own birds to ensure that they could identify them.

But bird ringing in its modern form is a relatively recent phenomenon, having been pioneered by a Dane, Christian Mortensen, who began the large-scale ringing of birds in 1899. The practice rapidly gained popularity amongst ornithologists throughout north-west Europe, and a further seven countries, including Great Britain, established official ringing schemes before the outbreak of the First World War in 1914.

The British schemes were the brainchild of two of the twentieth century's greatest ornithologists, H.F. (Harry) Witherby and Sir A. Landsborough Thomson. Thomson's scheme soon foundered, but Witherby's went from strength to strength, developing into today's national scheme run by the BTO.

Basically, bird ringing is a simple process. It involves catching the bird to be ringed, using a mist-net for smaller birds, and various forms of wire trap for larger ones. The captured bird is weighed, aged and sexed (where possible), and a small metal ring is placed around the lower part of one of its

Fair Isle Bird Observatory is a mecca for rare birds, thanks to the island's exposed position between Orkney and Shetland.

This 'Heligoland trap' is used to catch migrant birds for ringing.

legs, and fitted with a pair of specially-designed pliers. After ringing, the bird is normally released as soon as possible, to minimise any trauma or disturbance.

For smaller birds, the rings are made from aluminium and for larger birds, various alloys or steel. Each carries a unique serial number, together with an address to which the ring should be sent if the bird is found dead, or to which reports of re-trapped birds should be made.

The vast majority of birds are never seen again, but there are enough recoveries (normally ranging from below 1% for some songbirds to over 20% for waterfowl) to make bird ringing a vital tool in the study of bird movements and migration. Over the years, ringing has revealed the migration routes and winter destinations of many of our common summer visitors, and enabled ornithologists to advise conservation organisations on the best way to safeguard bird populations.

Ringing migrants such as this Knot provides valuable information about the species and its global journeys.

To become a Class A ringer you must undergo a long apprenticeship with a qualified ringer, lasting five years or more. Only then will you be given a licence enabling you to ring birds in your own right. There are only a thousand or so Class A ringers in the United Kingdom, so it's a tough challenge – but one that brings many rewards.

Seawatching needs a lot of patience: especially when there's not much to see!

A dream day for the seawatcher – loads of skuas, shearwaters and auks!

SEAWATCHING

Sooner or later, you'll find yourself sitting on a beach or coastal headland in a howling gale; wet, cold and fed up. Congratulations – you've become a seawatcher.

Seawatching doesn't have to be dull, pointless and mind-numbingly boring, but it often is. On the other hand, if you're lucky enough to be in the right place at the right time it can provide some of the most memorable birding experiences of your life.

The trick is to watch the weather. The real prize birds for the seawatcher – the ocean-going skuas, petrels and shearwaters – don't usually venture very near the coast. The exception is when passing weather fronts and strong onshore winds drive them to seek shelter close to land – providing the dedicated seawatcher the chance to get close-up views of rarely observed species.

September is the prime month for seawatching, especially off east coast promontories such as Flamborough and Filey, and the Cornish hotspots of Porthgwarra and St. Ives. When the birds' migration coincides with the right weather conditions, the results can be spectacular, as in the famous St. Ives' seawatch of 3rd September 1983, when almost every rare and unusual seabird on the British List passed by! But seabirds can turn up in the most unexpected conditions, such as the Black-browed Albatross off Dungeness during calm weather a year or two ago.

There is one way to cheat at seawatching, though it is sometimes frowned on by purists: the pelagic trip. Pelagics work on the simple principle that it's easier to go to the birds than wait for them to come to you.

Even a boat trip a mile or two offshore can bring you within reach of species like Sooty Shearwater and Pomarine Skua. Longer voyages out into the Western Approaches can provide a spectacular haul, including Sabine's Gull, Great and Cory's Shearwaters, and perhaps even the most sought-after seabirds of all, Wilson's and Fea's Petrels.

For those who prefer to stay within sight of shore, the RSPB run regular 'seabird cruises' off the Yorkshire port of Bridlington, which regularly provide sightings of the rarer shearwaters and skuas (*see* Further Information).

To see rare seabirds such as the Pomarine Skua may require many hours of dedicated seawatching.

Taking a boat trip around a seabird colony is the best way to get close-up views.

PHOTOGRAPHING BIRDS

One of the commonest questions asked of every birdwatcher is 'Do you photograph the birds you see?' It's almost as if people can't understand why you would want to watch birds if you couldn't keep a permanent visual record.

In fact, although many birders dabble in photography, very few take it up seriously. One reason is that the extra equipment is not only an added expense, but also more than doubles the weight you have to carry in the field. But the main deterrent is that when you photograph birds you often have to spend long periods of time in one place, waiting for a single bird to come close enough to capture on film. So to get one decent photo may take all day, during which you don't get much opportunity to watch any other birds!

Nevertheless, bird photography is a fascinating pastime in its own right, and even on a part-time basis can enhance your birding skills and knowledge.

As with all new skills, photographing birds takes time and patience. So it's best to start by spending a couple of hours in a place where the birds come reasonably close. You might try your local park, where ducks, coots and gulls can be attracted by the

Male Capercaillies occasionally attack anyone who ventures into their territory – even bird photographers!

provision of food. Or better still, why not cheat, and visit a collection of birds such as those at many Wildfowl and Wetlands Trust centres. You should be able to get close enough to take some really excellent pictures.

Take plenty of film, and use a longer lens than normal. If you're photographing captive birds, or those used to human presence, then something around 135–200 mm will do. But if you want to photograph wild birds, such as the birds that visit your garden feeding-station, you probably need a 400 mm or 500 mm, ideally a good quality one with a wide aperture.

Birds move very fast, so pick a bright day, fast film (e.g. 400 ISO), and mount your camera on a tripod to avoid shake. Use the fastest shutter-speed possible, and remember that although a bird can look quite near through the viewfinder, you may be disappointed when the prints come back to show a tiny dot in the centre of the frame!

If, having tried it out, you're serious about bird photography, then try to get advice from an experienced practitioner. You'll also need to consider how much you want to invest: with camera equipment, the sky is the limit.

If you take black-and-white photos, you may want to do your own developing and printing to get the best results. Colour slides

Getting a great action shot of an Osprey takes many hours of patience – and a lot of luck!

Keen bird photographers use expensive telephoto lenses to get closer to their quarry.

may be more useful especially if you want to give illustrated lectures, or sell your work to a magazine or agency.

One recent development has been the introduction of autofocus cameras and lenses. These are a godsend to the bird photographer, as one of the hardest things to get right is accurate focusing, especially when a bird is in flight. However, the autofocus can be very frustrating when trying to photograph a fast-moving bird, partially obscured by undergrowth; remember, you can always switch to manual!

It's also worth considering a course in the basics of photography. These can be at residential centres, such as those run by the Field Studies Council, or at your local Further Education College. All the better if you can find one that specialises in bird or nature photography.

Finally, remember that bird photography is expensive, and requires a lot more dedication than simply watching birds. Some highly skilled and dedicated people do manage to make a living from it, but when you first begin, don't give up the day job!

BIRDING ABROAD

Once you've been watching birds for a while in the British Isles, you may want to see what's on offer elsewhere. Maybe it's all those natural history films on television, or the colour illustrations in the field guides, but there's something very tempting about travelling abroad in search of new and exotic species.

So where should you go for your first foreign trip? Well, it makes sense to try a destination where at least some of the birds will be familiar ones, and for most people, a week or fortnight in France, the Netherlands or the Mediterranean is a good start.

Birds like the Hoopoe, a rare visitor to Britain, are commonplace over much of continental Europe, and most areas have their own speciality species, such as Eleonora's Falcon and Audouin's Gull in Mallorca, or Cyprus Warbler and Cyprus Pied Wheatear in – you've guessed it – Cyprus.

If you've only got a couple of weeks holiday a year, you may not be very popular with members of your family if you go off on your own on a specialist birding holiday.

Fortunately, you don't need to. Some of the best birding in Europe can be had on the doorstep of popular holiday resorts like the islands of Mallorca, Crete and Cyprus, the Spanish costas, or the Algarve in Portugal. Spring or autumn are the best times to visit, as these coincide with the peak migration seasons, but even in mid-summer there will always be some interesting birds.

If you're with family or friends, try not to spend the entire time staring through a pair of binoculars. Early morning and evening are usually the best times to watch birds, so devote these to birding and spend the rest of the time doing other things. By the end of the holiday you should find you've totted up an impressive list of species, and gained valuable experience of birds rarely seen at home.

Whether you're with your family or on your own, it's not always easy discovering where to go and what you're likely to see. So it's worth investing in a 'where to watch' guide, which either cover individual countries such as France, or areas like Eastern Europe. These offer a good general introduction to the birds

Although rare in Britain, the Hoopoe is a common sight on mainland Europe and around the Mediterranean.

Birders now travel the world in search of exotic birds – this group is visiting Bedaihe in eastern China.

you may encounter, and also give information about specific sites in a particular area.

However, they are sometimes out-of-date, and occasionally inaccurate. Better, if you can afford them, are the private trip reports produced by ordinary birders who have visited your chosen destination. These are available from the Foreign Birds Information and Reports Service (*see* Further Addresses).

Although you can go birding abroad on your own, one of the best ways to do so is with an organised bird tour – preferably run by one of the specialist bird holiday companies. These look expensive at first, but remember that the price generally includes everything except drinks, and you also get the benefit of expert leadership. This means that within a week or ten-day long tour you should manage to see most of the region's speciality species, and more importantly get really good views. You'll also gain the benefit of being with expert birders, and meet other like-minded enthusiasts.

Organised bird tours abroad range from a few days in western Europe, starting at around £700, to four weeks in Antarctica, for upwards of £5000. Just reading the catalogues produced by these companies can be a mouth-watering experience, and actually going on a tour can truly be the trip of a lifetime.

The Bee-eater is always a memorable bird to see on any foreign birding trip. This bird was photographed in Spain.

Birdwatching abroad is always a memorable experience, and when you return it's worth spending some time and effort writing up your sightings. This isn't just for your own benefit; a trip report can also be useful to anyone else who plans to visit the same area in the future.

A good trip report should include the following:

🐦 Dates of your visit.

🐦 A note on weather conditions.

🐦 A list of birding participants.

🐦 Locations you visited (with site directions and maps if possible).

🐦 A systematic list of the birds you saw: with dates, times (where relevant), numbers of birds, etc.

🐦 Field notes for particular species: especially birds you haven't seen before, local rarities, or unusual plumages, behaviour etc.

🐦 Line drawings and/or photographs if you have them.

Birding the easy way – watching rainforest species from a boat in Costa Rica!

5 THE BIGGER PICTURE

After you've been birding for a while, you begin to notice that there is more to the subject than questions of identification and behaviour. In this final chapter, I will explore some of the broader issues related to birds and birding. Some, like bird distribution, range and populations, are absolutely central to a birder's practical understanding of birds; others, such as bird names, or the place of birds in art, you can choose either to ignore, or investigate. What is clear is that birding can take you off in any direction you wish, from the significance of birds in classical music to the study of the history of the hobby. I shall also look at the connections between birding and conservation, and make suggestions as to how you can, if you wish, put something back into the pastime you enjoy so much.

DISTRIBUTION, POPULATION AND RANGE

To begin at the beginning: distribution and range – or to put it more simply, where birds live their daily lives. As one eminent ornithologist once said, 'A bird does not have a range... only a current range'. Bird populations and distribution change constantly – indeed to find a species whose population and range have stayed the same over any significant period (say twenty years or more) is a rare event. And a bird's distribution may also vary from year to year and season to season: many birds undertake short or long distance migrations, spending the summer in one area, and the winter in another.

Even during my relatively short lifetime, I have noticed major changes in the distribution and population of Britain's birds. When I was a lad, as they say, birds like the Bullfinch and Redpoll were a fairly regular sight, while I didn't see a Sparrowhawk or Hobby until my mid-teens, and a Peregrine even later. Now Sparrowhawks are a common sight in suburban London, while Hobbies have hugely increased in both numbers and range, and though still exciting to see, are no longer the rarity they once were.

Bullfinches are no longer the common sight they were when I was growing up during the 1970s.

Until relatively recently, I only saw Buzzards on a trip to the west country, Wales or Scotland. Nowadays they can be seen regularly along the M4, only a few miles outside London. All these birds of prey have benefited from a drop in persecution and the banning of chemicals such as DDT from the food chain.

Other species were virtually unknown when I was growing up. I saw my first Little Egret as a ten-year-old, on Brownsea Island in 1970; and didn't come across another in Britain for almost twenty years. Yet in the last decade or so they have become so common they barely warrant a second glance, especially along the south coast, and now breed in colonies

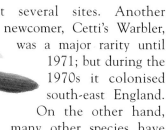

Cetti's Warbler was once a major rarity in Britain, but has now colonised as a regular breeding species.

at several sites. Another newcomer, Cetti's Warbler, was a major rarity until 1971; but during the 1970s it colonised south-east England. On the other hand, many other species have undergone major declines since I began birding. Who would have predicted, thirty years ago, that birds such as the Song Thrush, Starling and even the humble House Sparrow would give cause for concern? Modern farming methods, increased pollution from traffic, and piecemeal building on the countryside are all to blame; although ultimately the main culprit has been our own unwillingness or inability to fight social changes and political policies that have devastated our common bird populations.

Possibly we have turned the corner; now that bird populations have become part of the government's 'Quality of Life Index' there must surely be some hope. But today, birds face ever more varied threats, including possibly the biggest of them all, global climate change. Global warming has the potential to devastate habitats by changing them so rapidly that the ecosystems simply cannot cope. If that scenario comes to pass, then the lookout for many of our more specialised breeding species is poor indeed.

In contrast, the Grey Partridge has declined dramatically, mainly due to modern farming methods.

CONSERVATION ISSUES

So what can you do to help reverse the decline of our bird populations, and to help sustain them in the long term? Well, your first step should be to take an active part in conservation projects. Today you have many different options, of which the first two should be to join your local Wildlife Trust and the RSPB.

These two organisations act in a complementary way to safeguard the future of Britain's birds, habitats and other wildlife. On a global scale, the RSPB is investigating climate change and planning responses to it designed to preserve our country's biodiversity, and to save individually threatened species such as the Bittern. In doing so it has switched from its previously fairly passive, reactive approach to conservation, to a much more active one. So as well as buying up areas of excellent habitat such as Minsmere and Titchwell, and managing them as island reserves amidst a sea of poorer habitat, the RSPB is now buying up areas of land with potential, and creating new reserves from scratch.

Titchwell in Norfolk is the RSPB's most popular reserve, with over 140,000 visitors each year.

The Wildfowl & Wetlands Trust centre at Welney in Norfolk attracts huge numbers of wildfowl – and birders – every winter.

Bearded Tits are mainly confined to reedbeds, a habitat often found on RSPB and Wildlife Trust reserves.

The Wildlife Trusts are a diverse collection of local and regional organisations, each of which is committed to the active conservation and development of local habitats and their wildlife. They offer great opportunities to do something practical to help your local birds, along with all the fringe benefits of taking part in community projects, such as a varied social side and the opportunity to learn new skills. Many people who work full-time for both the RSPB and The Wildlife Trusts began doing so by volunteering, then progressed to something more permanent. Others are content to remain as volunteers, performing invaluable work on behalf of Britain's birds and other wildlife.

So if you want to put your effort where your mouth is, go along to your local Wildlife Trust or RSPB group and ask what you can do to help!

Another way of putting something back into birding, and getting more out of it, is to join the BTO (British Trust for Ornithology). Although this may sound like a very serious organisation, it welcomes new members, and encourages them to participate in a wide range of surveys and other projects designed to help us know more about Britain's birds.

The first step should be to join in the BTO's Garden BirdWatch; a long-running scheme in which all you have to do is to keep a regular record of the birds that come into your garden, to feed, breed or rest. This scheme has more than 10,000 active participants, and has taught us a vast amount about our commonest garden birds.

Once you feel confident about your ability to discover and identify a range of birds, you can also take part in other BTO surveys. Some for a specific species such as Skylarks or Rooks; others looking at the wider picture, such as the atlases of breeding and wintering birds, or the new 'Migration Atlas', which uses observations carried out by amateur birders all over Britain and Ireland to form a bigger picture of what is happening with our bird populations, distribution and range.

When you join the BTO you can take part in surveys of breeding birds such as Rooks.

Anyone who doubts the contribution made by ordinary birders to global conservation issues should look no further than the BTO's long-running Nest Record Scheme. A few years ago a BTO scientist analysed the nesting dates for many of our commoner breeding birds, using records from the scheme. He discovered that the majority of our common breeding species were nesting, and laying eggs, up to two weeks earlier than 30 years before; and were raising larger broods as a result. Further analysis proved that this could only be due to the effects of global warming; and indeed this finding was one of the first pieces of substantial proof that global climate change had definitely occurred. So next time someone asks you why you're giving up a morning's birding to take part in a BTO survey, you have a ready answer: because it really does make a difference.

Recent censuses have confirmed that the Tree Sparrow population has declined by almost 90%.

CLASSIFICATION AND TAXONOMY

Not every birder wants to get involved in conservation issues on a day-to-day basis. But as they make progress in their interest, it's hard to avoid getting drawn into other areas of ornithology, of which one of the most fascinating is the subject of bird classification and taxonomy.

Bird classification is, in essence, a form of archaeology: a search for the biologists' Holy Grail – a definitive account of the evolution of today's bird species, and the relationship between them. Unfortunately, just as with archaeology, much is inevitably based on educated guesswork, and mistakes undoubtedly occur. All we can really hope for is a 'best fit', in which we come as close as possible to understanding the history and development of the birds we love to watch.

It's worth spending some time getting to grips with bird classification, as it undoubtedly gives you a greater understanding of the birds you see. It works on a hierarchical system, in which a bird such as the Blackbird can be classified as follows:

Once thought to be two races of the same species, the Bean Goose (above) and Pink-footed Goose (below) are now considered full species in their own right.

 Class: Aves (birds).

 Order: Passeriformes (perching birds).

 Family: Turdidae (thrushes).

 Genus: Turdus (a group that includes Mistle and Song Thrushes).

 Specific name: Turdus merula (Common Blackbird).

Likewise, every bird (indeed every living organism known to man) has a two-part scientific name (a system known as binomial nomenclature), which in theory at least prevents confusion with any other species. So, for example, a Black Vulture in the Americas carries the scientific name *Coragyps atratus*, while its Eurasian counterpart, also often referred to as simply 'Black Vulture', has the scientific name *Aegypius monachus*.

Which order a bird belongs to generally reflects relationships which are clear to a field birder. So all perching birds come under the same order, Passeriformes, while ducks, geese and swans are grouped together in the order Anseriformes.

However, superficial similarities, due to a process known as convergent evolution, mean that herons and cranes are in different orders (Ciconiiformes and Gruiformes), and while herons' relatives include, as you might expect, storks and ibises, the relatives of cranes include such very different-looking species as rails and bustards!

Other orders range from those with only a handful of species in a single family, such as the Gaviiformes (divers), to the Charadriiformes, which comprises several hundred species from many families, including waders, gulls, terns and auks.

Most birders are familiar with the standard 'order of orders', starting with the Struthioniformes (Ostriches and their allies), and ending with the Passeriformes. However, recent work on the DNA of birds, pioneered by a group of American ornithologists, has turned this virtually upside-down.

The new classification shuffles the pack to place gamebirds next to wildfowl and pigeons and doves next to bustards, cranes and rails. It even moves some families into another order altogether! Thus the grebes become part of the Ciconiiformes, or long-legged wading birds.

This new work is still regarded by many as highly controversial, yet the pedigree of its authors deserves respect. Whether or not it will become accepted as the standard classification for the new millennium, we shall simply have to wait and see.

The so-called 'Yellow' Wagtail comes in a wide variety of different races, including the British 'Yellow Wagtail' (main picture) and the continental 'Blue-headed' (top).

Another confusing area of classification is the question of subspecies, or races.

It has been said that God made species, but man made subspecies. When he did so, he was storing up a whole lot of trouble for the future.

As the traveller-naturalists of the eighteenth and nineteenth centuries explored farther afield, they came across new populations of familiar species. Close observation showed that birds from these populations differed from the standard, or 'nominate' race. When these differences were held to be consistent, yet not so major as to allow the population to be ascribed to a new species, the birds concerned were labelled as a distinctive subspecies.

While our ornithological knowledge was confined to relatively few areas of the world, this was all well and good. But soon disagreements began to arise, with two rival camps emerging: the 'lumpers', who regarded variant populations as

relatively unimportant, and the 'splitters', who upgraded every minor variation to a new subspecies.

So over the years, the number of 'acceptable' different races of Yellow Wagtail has varied from around a dozen to as many as twenty! While some of these are certainly valid (and indeed may eventually prove to be separate species), others have been discovered to be merely hybrids or aberrant individuals, rather than 'proper' subspecies.

Occasionally, subspecies are 'upgraded' to become full species, at which point birdwatchers suddenly take a far greater interest in their status and distribution. For example, when I began birding in the late 1960s, Bean and Pink-footed Geese were still considered to be two distinctive races of the same species. Water and Rock Pipits had yet to be split, and many local bird reports failed to distinguish between them in their records.

Water Pipits (above) and Rock Pipits (below) were once considered to be the same species, despite major differences in breeding behaviour, habitat and plumage.

Yet the two highly distinctive forms of the Arctic Skua, pale and dark, are considered to be 'phases', rather than subspecies. This is because while they appear very different, the genetic differences between the two phases are very slight indeed. Moreover, unlike true subspecies, pale and dark forms are found throughout the birds' breeding range.

Today, many ornithologists have come to regard the subspecies as rather too rigid a concept for the real world. In reality, the characteristics of one population of birds tend to blur gradually into another, in what is known as a 'cline'. Frequent cross-breeding between two populations, and aberrant individuals, make it difficult, at times impossible, to assign a particular bird to a particular subspecies.

Nevertheless, in the coming years, as DNA testing becomes more and more sophisticated, we are likely to see another boom in the variety and number of subspecies being claimed. This raises an important question: if the birds can only be 'split' using sophisticated laboratory equipment, will the concept of 'subspecies' have any relevance to birdwatchers in the field?

BIRD NAMES AND THEIR ORIGINS

What's in a name? Why are some birds named after people (Pallas's Warbler) and others after places (Dartford Warbler)? Why are some named because of where they live (Marsh Tit), some by their size (Great Tit) and others by their colour (Blue Tit)? Why are all kinds of birds named after their *call* (Chiffchaff, Kittiwake, and so on), but not after their *smell*?!

Most species of birds were named by the people who first realised they were distinct species.

So it's hardly surprising that many birds are named after either a characteristic plumage feature (Red-throated Diver, Great Crested Grebe), their size (a whole host of littles, lessers and greaters), their habitat (Tree, Willow, Marsh, and so on) or their sound.

The Shorelark was named because of its winter habitat: sandy coasts.

The best-known onomatopoeic bird-names are Cuckoo, Chiffchaff and Kittiwake. But scratch the surface of many other names, and you'll find a reference to the bird's call. Our ancestors called the Chaffinch 'Pink' or 'Spink' because of its distinctive flight-call. Over the centuries, this gradually changed into the word 'finch', yet the original name has been preserved in the surname 'Spink', still found today in East Anglia and Yorkshire. Rook, Crow, Raven and even Turtle (as in Turtle Dove) are also derived from the birds' calls.

But beware! Not all bird names are as easy to understand as these; some are positively misleading. Wheatears have nothing to do with 'ears of wheat', the name literally means 'White-arse', and goes back to the days when 'arse' had no vulgar connections, and simply meant 'rump'.

The Razorbill was named because its beak looks like an old-fashioned, cut-throat razor.

For a newcomer to birding, learning the names of birds can be a real headache. There just doesn't seem to be any consistency! After all, why do most birds in the warbler family include the word 'warbler' in their name, while Whitethroat, Blackcap and Chiffchaff do not? Surely it would be more logical to standardise the names, and avoid confusion?

The Wheatear gets its name from an Anglo-Saxon phrase meaning 'white arse'!

Well, it's a nice idea, and like reforming English spelling, it's been around for a long time. But every time someone (generally a committee) tries it, the whole

The Black Redstart is known in Italy as the codirosso spazzocamino – meaning 'red-tailed chimney-sweep'!

The Kittiwake gets its name because of its distinctive call.

exercise begins to fall apart. This is because bird names are not handed down from above, but are part of our living language. They have evolved, and will continue to evolve, through common use, not just by birdwatchers and ornithologists, but in newspapers, on television and by the man or woman in the street.

Of course, bird names are far from permanent. Pick up any Victorian bird book and you'll find references to the 'Willow-Wren' (Willow Warbler) and 'Golden-crested Wren' (Goldcrest). These names fell out of use because they were misleading – rather like the way 'Hedge Sparrow' has recently been superseded by 'Dunnock'. But these changes happened over time, and not because a committee said so.

So to me, and to most people, the 'Sky Lark' will always be simply the Skylark, and no amount of pronouncements by committees, journals or august ornithological bodies will make us think otherwise.

BIRD ART, LITERATURE AND BOOKS

Birds, perhaps more than any other group of living creatures, have inspired generations of artists, musicians and writers. From Hieronymous Bosch to Picasso, John Keats to Ted Hughes, and Mozart to Messiaen, they have created work either expressly influenced or using images and sounds taken from the world of birds.

Many birders also have an interest in culture, and it can be fascinating to explore this world, enhanced by your new-found knowledge of birds. My personal favourite is the poetry of John Clare, who lived and wrote in rural Northamptonshire during the early nineteenth century. Clare's poetry and prose are packed with references to birds and birdsong, and for me he evokes the true spirit of birds better than any other writer, dead or alive, as in these lines from 'The Sky Lark':

'...*up the skylark flies*
And oer her half formed nest with happy wings
Winnows the air – till in the clouds she sings
Then hangs a dust spot in the sunny skies
And drops and drops till in her nest she lies...'

The Skylark has inspired poets more than any other bird apart, perhaps, from the Nightingale.

I challenge anyone to look at a singing skylark in the same way again after reading Clare's magnificent poetry.

Bird books are another joy the new birder soon discovers. Some people can pass a bookshop by; others will always want to take a look, often heading straight for the natural history section. Today's bird books are so wide-ranging in scope and subject that you can find one on almost anything – although you may struggle to find something readable! If you want to enter into the spirit of birding, and read some highly entertaining books, I suggest the following list, in order of their original date of publication:

The Natural History of Selborne by Gilbert White (1789). The first popular book about British birds, and still readable and relevant today.

Wild America by James Fisher and Roger Tory Peterson (1955). An extraordinary travelogue across the continent by the top English and American birders of their day.

Adventure Lit their Star by Kenneth Allsop (1962). A novel about the colonisation of Britain by the Little Ringed Plover. Quirky but fascinating.

Collecting out-of-print bird books can be a very rewarding and fascinating hobby.

The Shell Bird Book by James Fisher (1966). In my opinion, still the best book on birds ever written, with an entertaining, readable text full of erudition, as you would expect from a great populariser.

An Eye for a Bird by Eric Hosking with Frank W. Lane (1970). The autobiography of the first modern bird photographer.

Bill Oddie's Little Black Bird Book by Bill Oddie (1980). The ultimate 'insider job' on why we watch birds! Brilliantly funny and accurate. (See all Bill Oddie's other autobiographical works, too).

Biographies for Birdwatchers by Barbara and Richard Mearns (1988). The lives of those men and women commemorated in Western Palearctic bird names. A great fireside read.

The Minds of Birds by Alexander Skutch (1996). Do birds think, feel and play? The result of a lifetime's close observation of birds by a nonagenarian ornithologist, based in Central America.

The Great Auk by Errol Fuller (1999). An eccentric yet un-put-downable work, containing everything you ever wanted to know (and a lot you never knew you did!) about this long-lost bird. (See the same author's *Extinct Birds* (2000)).

Birders – Tales of a Tribe by Mark Cocker (2001). A thoughtful, witty and often moving account of why we watch birds.

You may find that many of these and related works are now out of print, though by carefully searching second-hand bookshops or bookfairs you will probably come across most of them.

THE FUTURE OF BIRDING

No one who has been birding for the last couple of decades can fail to have noticed the extraordinary changes that have taken place during that time.

Some have been for the better. Improvements in optical equipment, field guides and identification techniques, and easier access to the world's birding hotspots have all done much to transform a minority interest into one of Britain's fastest-growing leisure activities. Birding may not yet be 'the new rock'n'roll', but it can surely only be a matter of time!

Some changes, on the other hand, have been for the worse. The obsession with arcane points of identification and rarity hunting, sometimes at the expense of the study and enjoyment of common birds, has not always been welcome. Much more seriously, the continued decline of bird populations at home and abroad, as a result of changes in land use, persecution and habitat loss, has been far more severe than we could have imagined back in the 1960s and 1970s.

In the last few years, we have seen the arrival on the scene of two factors, which threaten to change beyond recognition, both the science of ornithology, and the pastime of birding. The first is the rise of the 'new taxonomy', in which revolutionary biological techniques are beginning to overturn our concept of what constitutes different species. The second is the spectre of

This young birder will see some dramatic changes during his lifetime.

global climate change, surely the most serious long-term threat facing the world's birds.

So what of the next 30 or so years? Time to get out the crystal ball and make some serious – and not quite so serious – predictions about birding in the first quarter of the twenty-first century...

The Snowy Owl has already become extinct as a British breeding bird, possibly as a result of global warming.

- Optics will continue to improve, with image stabilisers and auto-focus becoming standard in bins and scopes. At the same time, new lightweight materials will make sore necks a thing of the past.

- Hand in hand with the improvement in visual aids, bird identification will continue to progress by leaps and bounds. Eventually, a field guide with every British and European species will be available on a hand-held computer.

- As Britain's traffic begins to grind to a permanent halt, the importance of local patches will assume crucial significance, while because of the gridlock, twitching will rapidly decline.

- To overcome their inability to travel, birders will use digital video cameras to record their local sightings, displaying them on the Internet. Instead of life lists, birders will compete to have the most comprehensive website.

- British bird names will gradually simplify, as more and more people get fed up typing long words into their computer.

Changes in weather patterns, as a result of global warming, could bring more scarce migrants such as this Bluethroat to our shores.

- As a result of Global Warming, the following species will become extinct: anything with 'Snow' in its name, all migrants, all habitat specialists, all shore nesters, and any bird requiring more than six inches of water. Winners in the climate change lottery will be alien species, gulls, crows and pigeons, which can easily adapt to the new conditions.

- John Smith (not his real name), from North London, will become the last person in Britain who does not feed the birds in his garden. Prosecuted under the new 'Garden Bird Support Act', he will be sentenced to be pecked to death by a flock of hungry Blue Tits.

- If current trends continue, The Wildlife Trusts will celebrate its ten millionth member by the year 2010, and include the entire United Kingdom population by the year 2050. At that year's General Election, there will be a landslide majority for the New Birder Party – symbol, a red Robin.

WHY WATCH BIRDS?

So after reading this book, and hopefully only skipping one or two bits, the question I posed at the beginning should be even more applicable: why watch birds? All the usual reasons given in chapter one are still relevant – but hopefully you will have found a reason, or reasons, of your own. Some may be purely personal, others more altruistic, but one thing is sure. If you've got this far, then you're well and truly hooked, a birder quite literally for life. I hope you enjoy it as much as I have, do and will, until my last day on Earth.

Starlings gathering to roost at Brighton's west Pier – proving that even common birds in familiar places can be memorable and exciting!

USEFUL ADDRESSES

British Birdwatching Fair Office
Fishponds Cottage, Hambleton Road, Oakham
Rutland LE15 8AB
www.birdfair.org.uk

If you want to get involved in census work, write to the
BTO (British Trust for Ornithology)
The National Centre for Ornithology, The Nunnery
Thetford, Norfolk IP24 2PU
Tel: 01842 750050
www.bto.org.uk
The BTO offers birdwatchers the opportunity to learn
more about birds by taking part in surveys such as the
Garden BirdWatch or the Nest Record Scheme. BTO
members also receive a bi-monthly magazine, *BTO News*.

CJ Wildbird Foods Ltd
The Rea, Upton Magna, Shrewsbury SY4 4UB
Tel: 0800 731 2820 (Freephone)
www.birdfood.co.uk
CJ Wildbird Foods is Britain's leading supplier of bird
feeders and foodstuffs, via mail order. The company
sponsors the BTO Garden BirdWatch survey, and also
produce a free handbook of garden feeding, containing
advice on feeding garden birds, and a catalogue of products.

Foreign Birds Information and Reports Service
6 Skipton Crescent, Berkeley Pendlesham
Worcester WR4 0LG
Tel: 01905 454541

RSPB (Royal Society for the Protection of Birds)
The Lodge, Sandy, Bedfordshire SG19 2DL
Tel: 01767 680551
www.rspb.org.uk
The RSPB is Britain's leading bird conservation
organisation, with almost one million members. It runs
more than 100 bird reserves up and down the country,
and has a national network of members' groups. Members
receive four copies of *Birds* magazine each year, while new
members receive a gift on joining. The junior arm of the
RSPB, the Young Ornithologists Club (YOC), is for
members up to the age of sixteen.

Subbuteo Natural History Books Ltd
The Rea, Upton Magna, Shrewsbury SY4 4UB
Tel: 0870 010 9700
Email: sales@subbooks.demon.co.uk
Subbuteo Books provides a fast, helpful and reliable mail
order service for books on birds and other aspects of
natural history, including those on garden birds. Free
catalogue available on request.

WWT (Wildfowl & Wetlands Trust)
Slimbridge, Gloucestershire GL2 7BT
Tel: 01453 891900
www.wwt.org.uk
The WWT is primarily dedicated to conservation of the
world's wetlands and their birds. It runs nine centres in

the UK, including the new Wetland Centre in Barnes,
west London, and the famous headquarters at Slimbridge
in Gloucestershire. Members receive a quarterly magazine,
Wildfowl & Wetlands, and get free entry to WWT centres.

The Wildlife Trusts
The Kiln, Waterside, Mather Road
Newark, Nottinghamshire NG24 1WT
Tel: 0870 036 7711
www.wildlifetrusts.org
See page 5 for information.

Wildsounds
Dept HTWB, Cross Street, Salthouse
Norfolk NR25 7XH
Tel: 01263 741100
www.wildsounds.com
Wildsounds is Britain's leading supplier of birdsong tapes
and CDs, including several on garden birds. They also
stock a range of 'Teach Yourself' products, particularly
useful for the beginner.

NATIONAL BIRDLINE
Latest news 09068 700222
(phone in sightings 01263 741140)

REGIONAL BIRDLINES
Birdline East Anglia
Latest news 09068 700245
(phone in sightings 0800 083 0803)

Birdline South East
Latest news 09068 700240
(phone in sightings 0800 037 7240)

Birdline South West
Latest news 09068 700241
(phone in sightings 0800 037 7241)

Birdline North East
Latest news 09068 700246
(phone in sightings 07626 983963)

Birdline North West
Latest news 09068 700249
(phone in sightings 0151 336 6188)

Birdline Midlands
Latest news 09068 700247
(phone in sightings 01905 754154)

Birdline Scotland
Latest news 09068 700234
(phone in sightings 01292 611994)

Birdline Wales
Latest news 09068 700248
(phone in sightings 01492 544588)

Birdline Northern Ireland
Latest news 0289 146 7408

FURTHER READING

Attracting Birds to Your Garden
by Stephen Moss & David Cottridge
(New Holland, 1998)

Bill Oddie's Birds of Britain and Ireland
by Bill Oddie (New Holland, 1998)

Bill Oddie's Introduction to Birdwatching
by Bill Oddie (New Holland, 2002)

Birds of Europe
by Lars Jonsson (A&C Black, 1996)

Birdwatcher's Pocket Field Guide
by Mark Golley (New Holland, 2003)

Collins Bird Guide
by Lars Svensson, Peter Grant, Killian Mullarney
& Dan Zetterstrom (Collins, 2001)

Collins Field Guide to Bird Songs and Calls
by Geoff Sample (Collins, 1996)

The Complete Garden Bird Book
by Mark Golley, Stephen Moss & David Daly
(New Holland, 1996)

The Garden Bird Year
by Roy Beddard & Dave Daly
(New Holland, 2001)

The Pocket Guide to Birds of Britain and North-West Europe
by Chris Kightley, Steve Madge & Dave Nurney
(Pica Press, 1998)

Magazines and other publications

BBC Wildlife
Available monthly from newsagents, or by
subscription from:
**BBC Wildlife Subscriptions, PO Box 279
Sittingbourne, Kent ME9 8DF
Tel: 01795 414718**

Birdwatch
Available monthly from larger newsagents, or by
subscription from:
**Warners, West Street, Bourne, Lincolnshire PE10 9PH
Tel: 01778 392027
www.birdwatch.co.uk**

The Birdwatcher's Yearbook
Available annually in October, price around £15, from:
**55 Thorpe Park Road, Peterborough PE3 6LJ
Tel: 01733 561739**

Birdwatching
Available monthly from larger newsagents, or by
subscription from:
**Bretton Court, Peterborough PE3 8DZ
Tel: 01733 264666**

British Birds
Available monthly by subscription only from:
**The Banks, Mountfield, Robertsbridge,
East Sussex TN32 5JY
Tel: 01580 882039
subscriptions@britishbirds.co.uk
www.britishbirds.co.uk**

ACKNOWLEDGEMENTS

This book is not only the product of almost forty years interest in birds, but also of more than thirty years spent in the field with friends and companions. In roughly chronological order, I should like to thank Daniel Osorio, with whom I spent many happy days birding back in the 1970s, and who still accompanies me on trips today; Neil McKillop, with whom I have watched birds throughout Britain and abroad; and my son James, who used to come with me to visit my local patch, and may still harbour a latent interest in birds! I should also like to thank the following people who come birding with me: Bill Oddie, Nigel Bean, Nigel and Cheryle Redman, Jackie Follett, Graham Coster, and Rod Standing and his son Daniel, whose enthusiasm at an early age fills me with optimism for the next generation of birders.

Thanks too to Jo Hemmings and Camilla MacWhannell at New Holland, David Tipling for his excellent photographs, and David Daly for his delightful illustrations.

Parts of this book originally appeared in a series of articles, 'First Principles', in Birdwatch magazine. I am grateful to the magazine's editor, Dominic Mitchell, for allowing me to republish this material here.

Finally, to my wife Suzanne, who I met on a field trip at Juniper Hall in Surrey, and who has since been by my side while birding in Britain and abroad – my eternal gratitude.

INDEX